CRAZY HORSE AND THREE STARS

David Wiltse

BROADWAY PLAY PUBLISHING INC
New York
www.broadwayplaypublishing.com
info@broadwayplaypublishing.com

First printing: October 2010
I S B N: 978-0-88145-416-1

Book design: Marie Donovan
Typographic controls: Adobe InDesign
Typeface: Palatino
Printed and bound in the U S A

ABOUT THE AUTHOR

David Wiltse is the author of twelve novels and
twelve plays. he is the recipient of an N E A grant for
SEDITION and has also been awarded the Drama
Desk Award for "Most Promising Playwright", and
an Edgar Allan Poe Award for other works. Mr Wiltse
was formerly the Playwright-in-Residence at the
Westport Country Playhouse in Westport, Connecticut.

CRAZY HORSE AND THREE STARS was first produced by Long Whart Theater (Arvin Brown, Artistic Director; M Edgar Rosenblum, Executive Director), opening on 24 January 1992. The cast and creative contributors were:

CRAZY HORSE ....Barry Mulholland
GENERAL CROOK ....Frank Converse
LIEUTENANT CLARK .... James Andreassi
GRUARD... Tracy Griswold
WITNAKE ....Machisté
SOLDIER/SPIRIT...................................... Matthew Burnett

Director.. Mark Brokaw
Unit set design..Hugh Landwehr
Set coordination & properties ....David Fletcher
Costume coordination ....Patricia M Risser
Lighting...Jay Strevey
Sound ....Brenton Evans
Script development ....Sari Bodi & James Luse
Production stage manager ....Ruth M Feldman

CHARACTERS & SETTING

CRAZY HORSE, *war chief of the Lakota, thirties*
WITNAKE, *his cousin and contemporary*
GENERAL CROOK, *American soldier, late fifties*
LIEUTENANT CLARK, CROOK's *adjutant, thirties*
GRUARD, *American scout, forties*
SOLDIER, *various roles*

SPIRITS, SOLDIERS, *etc, if needed*

The action takes place in the mountains, woods, and plains of the American West, 1876-77.

N B

The scenery of this play is to be representational, relying on lights, projections, scrims, drop-cloths, etc, depending entirely upon availability and the imaginations and conceptions of the director and designer.

Suggestions have been made as to the staging of various scenes, but these are only suggestions and will naturally be altered by the means of production at hand.

Although the production can be starkly simple or very elaborate, the play was conceived and written to be performed on a virtually bare stage, with one scene flowing rapidly into the next.

Neither Indians nor Whites should speak with accents.

ACT ONE

(At rise: Music is heard briefly, featuring the feel of atonal Amerindian music, but not literally any of their chants. The overall effect should be one of mystery, an alien culture to European ears, with the hint of threat implied by the unknown.)

(CRAZY HORSE is discovered center stage in a trance-like state. He is dressed simply and has just emerged from a sweat lodge. He stands with eyes closed, head tilted backwards as if he were receiving a message from on high.)

(Spirit Figures appear behind and above CRAZY HORSE, looking down on him. Spirit Figures represent the Great Powers of the four directions. Their bodies are painted red with black lightning streaks, yellow with black lightning, black with blue lightning and white with red lightning. The Spirits begin a chant, a rythmic grunting in which no real words are spoken.)

(An eagle shrieks, and then is seen flying over CRAZY HORSE. This is CRAZY HORSE's totem, a creature with special powers for him. CRAZY HORSE reaches upwards and makes a brief, ecstatic, wordless sound.)

(CRAZY HORSE ascends a rise so that he is level with the Spirit Figures. Still chanting, they approach him. CRAZY HORSE contines to look sightlessly skyward. The figures begin to dress CRAZY HORSE in ceremonial garb, as formally as if they were preparing a priest, or a king for coronation.)

Among the vestments is a cape made of black and white colt hide.)

CRAZY HORSE: I am Crazy Horse. The eagle shall lead me, the bear shall be my strength. Join me, Lakotah and Cheyenne! We shall drive the Wasichu from the lands given us by the Great Powers and our fathers' spirits. We shall thrust away the burning cup of alcohol that enfeebles the mind and enslaves the soul with a thirst that can not be quenched. Before the Wasichus came we had no wants that were not fulfilled, we had not need of them and their liquid fire. Now the once feared Red Cloud stands with his hand out, begging for food. The young men lie about the agency, seeking permission to hunt, permission to ride. Our own children need no permission, shall our warriors seek it? Come with me, we shall leave the agency forever. I have been given a vision. No bullet can pierce my flesh. I shall never shake the hand of the Wasichu until he is gone from our land. I shall live for The People and see them through this darkness to the light. Our ways will be ways of the Lakota, the old ways, the sacred ways. We shall return to the Wasichu his blankets and his beads and his beef. And if he comes again within our land, we shall return his bullets! If they raise a hand against us, they shall die!

(Music, a fantasy on military marches of the time, is heard. The music is not quite as we know it, but as it would be perceived by a different culture at the time. It is familiar, but not the same. With the music comes a swirl of high winds, lightning, thunder. The stage is semi-dark, lighted by flashes of lightning that come from above, behind, and sometimes almost from the hands of CRAZY HORSE.)

(Enter blond general and SOLDIERS, turning, bewildered and confused, blown on by the storm which is not merely a storm. The SOLDIERS wear the U S Army uniforms of the time, the blond general sports long blond hair to his

*shoulders and wears a buckskin shirt over army pants. The
chanting of the Figures continues and becomes more frenzied
with the action. The Figures continue to dress* CRAZY
HORSE *and each new adornment brings about an increased
intensity in the action.)*

(Shots and cries. The SOLDIERS *realize they are under attack.
They look up and see: more Indians appear on the rise on
either side of but somewhat lower than* CRAZY HORSE *and
the Figures. The Indians brandish bows and tomahawks
and rifles, but do not actually aim them at the Soldiers. The
soldiers lift their weapons to fire. The Figures put a beaded
vest on the chest of* CRAZY HORSE. *The* SOLDIERS *fire but
hit no one.* CRAZY HORSE *now gestures first left and then
right, as if directing his men into battle. The Indians respond
by gestures of their own towards the Soldiers.* WITNAKE *is
among the Indian warriors. The battle continues briefly until
the Figures put the final adornment on* CRAZY HORSE, *the
buffalo helmet. Now fully attired, fully empowered,* CRAZY
HORSE *lifts his arms so they extend over the* SOLDIERS. *Like
a magician, he makes another sound. In one hand he holds
a bear claw. In another an eagle's wing. The* SOLDIERS *and
General fall dead. the General going last. The shriek of the
eagle is heard again, and once more it flies above* CRAZY
HORSE.)*

(The stage has been dimly lighted except for CRAZY HORSE.
Now it goes dark except for CRAZY HORSE *who stands alone
in a spot. The chanting stops, the storm is over, the music
gone.* CRAZY HORSE *stares regally forward, no longer in a
trance, but a man very much in command of all his powers.)*

(The eagle shrieks, the Indians cry out exultantly. Black out)

*(Martial music, this time funereal in tone. It is muted.
Enter* GENERAL CROOK, LIEUTENANT CLARK. CLARK
*carries a campaign chair which he immediately unfolds so
that* CROOK *can sit.* CROOK *ignores the chair for a moment,
although he would love to sit.)*

CROOK: Here?

CLARK: Yes sir, here upon this hill. We found their bodies where they fell, packed so close together they died in each other's arms like true comrades.

CROOK: Each using another's corpse as shield, no doubt.... Were the bodies mutilated?

CLARK: All but three.

CROOK: The squaws are avid in their work. Did Custer keep his hair?

CLARK: He was untouched.

CROOK: A nice gesture. Someone has respect for command... So cramped a place to hold two hundred souls beneath my feet.

CLARK: Surely their souls are in heaven, sir.

CROOK: Do you believe so? Well, they are in heaven, then, and surely grateful to those who sent them there. Custer, was he atop this pile of comrades?

CLARK: No, sir. In the heart.

CROOK: Then perhaps he did not live to see his folly in full.

CLARK: Surely no man was braver, sir.

CROOK: No doubt, and none deader now. War is not about brave men. Courage was served by the cannon-full in the war just past. I have seen valor turn a skirmish—it will not win a war. Give me numbers and weapons that fire and cede the others all the heart in the world. Even the lion hunts in prides; alone, mere hyenas wear him down.

CLARK: Would you care to sit, sir? Are you tired?

CROOK: (*Ruefully*) I am not so infirm as I look.

CLARK: We were told you have a leg....

CROOK: Solicit me if I complain.... Sorry, lad. Five hours astride that mule has worn my manners thin.

CLARK: I just want to say, sir, you came on us so quick we had not time to welcome you formally. We are all so proud to serve with you.... They say you subdued the Paiutes and the Apache.

CROOK: I helped to free those tribes.

CLARK: Free them? Surely they were free before you brought them to reservations.

CROOK: They were, as beasts are free, which is shackled by unyielding custom, each man doomed to live the same life as his father, each woman doomed to worse. I brought them civilization and freed them from the cage of history.

CLARK: The mounts and deserts of Arizona are such a long way from here.

CROOK: It is a land God made in anger and the people there do thrive on spite.

CLARK: (*Admiringly*) They tell us you knew the Apache chief, Geronimo.

CROOK: A sour man, a malcontent, little loved among his people. He was no leader, only a bandit.

CLARK: They say Geronimo...

CROOK: Too much is made of the man!

CLARK: Yes, sir.

CROOK: The Apaches are a thousand miles from here, let us leave them there. In my saddlebag is a copy of Gibbon. fetch it for me. We have much to do and must depart within the hour—yet stolen moments are most precious... And my head scout—how is he called?

CLARK: Gruard.

CROOK: Fetch him first.

CLARK: Sir...if I may.

(CROOK *nods assent.*)

CLARK: I would be wary of the man. He shows little respect and holds nothing dear, save his own life.

CROOK: He sounds a man of the times.

CLARK: The subject of fornication seems much on his mind, though at the oddest times; and even that he treats as comedy.

CROOK: (*Amused*) That is oft the safest way.

CLARK: He will not meet my gaze at times and yet again he will stare overlong as if all candor lies within his eyes.

CROOK: (*Amused*) You have made a study of the man. Does he also scout awhile?

CLARK: He is an excellent scout. They say he has lived among the Sioux—with a squaw for wife.

CROOK: A sensible arrangement. Fetch him, then let us speak alone awhile.

(CLARK *exits. Only now that he's alone does* CROOK *allow himself to sit, easing down with caution and some pain, stretching one leg out in front of him. This sciatic leg will bother him throughout the play; although he will try not to give in to it he must eventually rub it, shift weight from it, etc, in unavailing efforts to ease the ache.*)

CROOK: I know the man the Spaniards call Geronimo...
     Three thousand Apache now till the land because of me. They do not raid, they do not kill, they practice honest husbandry—and one roams free. Three thousand for civility, one who will not bend—and men speak only of him. I have the numbers, he the name....
I know Geronimo. I know him as the Indian knows the buffalo for I have stalked and studied him, smelled his scent from afar. I have sweltered with him in the

summer sun and frozen with him in the desert night
as chill as an ice house. I have held his horse's dung
between my fingers to gauge the hour of his passing
and I have caught his musk on the downwind breeze.
I have felt his fear as the hunter closed in and sensed
his taunting laughter tinkling like birdsong when he
eluded me. I have slept at night when the sweat of
chasing him had dried to a crust of salt that cut my
skin.

I have carved no image of Geronimo but I have
painted him on the skins of my mind as clearly as the
Apache draws in sand his favored prey, with respect,
with reverence, with the keen blood lust of a man
yearning for the feast. Hate him? Man, I would kill him
with my teeth.

*(During this speech, CLARK enters with book and stands
apart, out of earshot of CROOK. FRANK GRUARD, the scout,
enters and stands with CLARK, regarding CROOK. GRUARD
is dressed in a motley of old, serviceable garments. His boots
are Indian.)*

GRUARD: Is this the man the Lakota call Three Stars and
the Apaches named Grey Wolf? Old Dog, more like.
What do you make of him?

CLARK: He seems troubled. Still, they say he made
gardeners of the Apaches. He tamed Geronimo.

GRUARD: Tamed him? He escorted him in. and when
the heathen wished, he left again. Crook could not
keep the devil chained.

CLARK: I'm sure he's a great man. Everyone says...But
I saw Custer. He wore glory like epaulettes upon his
shoulders and when he rode amongst the heathen the
very luster of the man was enough to fright the savage.
Yet this man thinks him a fool.

GRUARD: Never choose your heroes among the living,
they may live to disappoint.

CLARK: He would read of the fall of Rome while Custer's wounds cry out for vengeance. I would our hands were scarlet to the elbows now.

GRUARD: Boy, your energy fatigues me. Go at a woman like that and you'll be spent before she knows you started. You must pace yourself with slow reserve and let matters build as they will or she'll be left to battle on alone.

CLARK: I was speaking not of women, I know how to deal with women well enough.

GRUARD: You're heard about it, have you?

CLARK: I have some knowledge—I have not made it my life's work.

GRUARD: It is the work of life, old son. I know no better way to procreate than with a woman and a favoring moon, but as with anything, you have to like the work for its own sake.

(GRUARD *starts towards* CROOK, CLARK *stops him, gives him the copy of Gibbon.*)

CLARK: His Gibbon.

(CLARK *exits;* GRUARD *crosses to* CROOK.)

GRUARD: You fetched me?

CROOK: (*Surprised*) You move quietly, Gruard. (*He gets to his feet, not to be seen as infirm.*) We're standing in an abbatoir. I wanted the company of someone experienced with burying men.

GRUARD: I have some.

CROOK: You have the look. My lieutenant has only heard of death from a far place and the rumor has gained finery in its passage. He finds some glint of glory in it. He may resent that I do not offer a lance to hurl himself upon. I do not trust glorious men, Gruard. Are you eager to die?

GRUARD: I have a terrible fear of dying. I've seen too many men who didn't care for it. On the other hand, I've heard no complaints about being dead.

CROOK: I have heard of a Gruard from New York State. He had a squaw and a half-breed child and lived with the Sioux for many years. Are you that Gruard?

GRUARD: I was that man. The squaw and the child are gone—and that man with them.

CROOK: I am sorry.

GRUARD: A trifling matter—a squaw and a breed and fifteen years of life. (*Pause; lightly*) It is past.

CROOK: ...What is this place?

GRUARD: The People know that stream as Greasy Grass.

CROOK: Who were they who did this?

GRUARD: They call themselves The People, which makes the rest of us not quite up to the mark. I find that a mite insulting, but I never told one to his face.

CROOK: A common arrogance. The Apache named themselves Tinneh, the Human Beings. Their neighbors called them Apache, which means "the enemy". Both were apt.

GRUARD: These were Lakotah, different bands, Hunkpapa, Minniconjou, Oglalla, and a sprinkling of Cheyenne, happy to add their bit of vengeance. They were led by Sitting Bull and Gall and a saint they call Crazy Horse.

CROOK: A saint? Religion is thick in the air.

GRUARD: They say no bullet can tear his flesh. And they believe it.

CROOK: Do you believe, scout?

GRUARD: I believe none can until it does, but pay no heed to me. I might have said the other one did not walk on water except in deepest winter.

CROOK: You are blashpemous, Scout.

GRUARD: Only when asked, sir.

CROOK: ...We will start with Crazy Horse, then. One wild stallion can tempt the docile herd. We shall bring this saint into the fold, Gruard.

GRUARD: We can try. They may hold a different opinion. I guess them to be twenty thousand strong.

CROOK: The Sioux have doomed themselves, Scout. This battle was their death knell.

GRUARD: We lost two hundred and twenty-five men, General. The Sioux lost three, or so they boast. It will take some time to whittle down twenty thousand, three at a go.

CROOK: Do you know your recent history, Scout? In the insurrection just past brilliant, brassy Bobby Lee took all his battles. And poor Grant, dull and plodding, lost and bled until he won the war. The Sioux have massed themselves, Gruard. They will not survive it. They lack the supplies, they lack the fodder, the food, the weapons. The Indian is a warrior, not a soldier. He knows how to fight, not wage war. I will bring him a kind of contest he has not seen and will not comprehend. This is his summer, his time of glory. He lives in plenty, and we will not challenge him direct, but: we will dog him. When the weather turns and the grass for his ponies grows sere and he splits into bands—we will be there. Let him exult now—but let him fear the winter.... Give me the status of our scouts, their tribe and strength.

GRUARD: We have Crow warriors, some hundred or two, who were born in hatred of the Sioux.

CROOK: It will not do. I want Lakotah scouts. I need the Sioux to fight the Sioux.

GRUARD: The Crow will kill them as dead.

CROOK: I do not come to kill the Sioux, Gruard. I come to pacify him. He wars against the inevitable and spends his energy in profligate hate of progress. A new world awaits the Indian and we are but the shadow that precedes it. He flees from shadows now but must be taught to recognize the substance that casts them forth. First comes peace, then education, then participation. He has both courage and spirit; I do not seek to break them but to give them new direction. For this purpose I need scouts who know him best.

GRUARD: The Sioux will not scout for you against his own.

CROOK: He will.

GRUARD: None that I know. He is too proud. Why should he?

CROOK: It will be in his own interests. Ultimately every man serves his own needs—if he's thinking rightly. We will show the Sioux a new way to think.

GRUARD: You want me to find a traitor.

CROOK: Find a man who's wise enough to know which way the wind is blowing...It is a fair wind for him, Scout. In the long run.

(CROOK and GRUARD *exit. A swirl of music, the scenery changes, and we are in a Sioux encampment.* CRAZY HORSE *stands in a kind of trance with spirit figures. Enter* WITNAKE. CRAZY HORSE *is startled by his approach and grabs a lance and threatens* WITNAKE *before realizing who he is. Spirits vanish.)*

WITNAKE: Cousin!

CRAZY HORSE: (*Coming to himself*) Forgive me. I thought you were a demon.

WITNAKE: A demon? I?

CRAZY HORSE: I see them often. Do you not?

WITNAKE: No.

CRAZY HORSE: It is not given to every man to know them. Like women, the spirits have their favorites, no man knows why.

WITNAKE: Perhaps they find the purer souls.

CRAZY HORSE: Perhaps.

WITNAKE: I would be afrighted by such visitors.

CRAZY HORSE: I am accustomed to terror, Witnake. It is a price I must pay to keep these demons from the People.

WITNAKE: You are too much alone. You should join your people. This is a time of joy, come rejoice with us, don't keep yourself always so much apart, cousin. You set your lodge too far from the others.

CRAZY HORSE: Is it for you to judge my purpose? I am solitary that the demons can find only me... Why do you visit me?

WITNAKE: I have brought you a demon of a different kind. You know this one's name. He is Yugata who calls himself Frank Gruard. He scouts now for the Wasichu with three stars on his shoulder. He comes to us with this Three Stars's offer of "peace." He must be crazy.

CRAZY HORSE: They are all crazy who scout for the soldiers. The insolent Crow now take Wasichu beef and blankets to hunt us...

WITNAKE: But the Crow have always been our enemies. We have destroyed many Crow together, and will again.

CRAZY HORSE: Not in the company of soldiers. We will not ask the Wasichu to kill for us.

WITNAKE: (*Shrugs*) I despise the Crow, but not more because they scout for Three Stars.

CRAZY HORSE: You are forgiving.

WITNAKE: No man hates them more! ...But it is their nature to fight us. I do not blame a thing for following its nature. And if he receives blankets and beef and rifles for his nature...he is a sensible man.

CRAZY HORSE: You are too practical for my liking. Do you not blame a thing for betraying its own kind?

WITNAKE: Its own kind? The Crow is not of my kind! They say they sleep with their mothers, they say they eat their own young. I have hated the Crow all my life, as have you, we were born to hate them, it is in the order of things.

CRAZY HORSE: Would you scout for the Wasichu against the Crow?

WITNAKE: To kill a Crow and take his ponies I would even scout for your demons.

CRAZY HORSE: Do not speak lightly of my demons until you have faced them, cousin. The Crow seek but to kill us; the Wasichu to change our ways. That is the greater fear.... Bring in Yugata.

(WITNAKE *exits.*)

CRAZY HORSE: (*Chanting to four directions*) Hey! Hey! Hey! Hey! Hear me Grandfathers! Why do you send me such dreams? Why do you torment me with these demons? What shall I do? The People are brave, but weak in understanding, like an infant who shakes his

fist and yells at the ravening wolf, his courage fed by
ignorance. He does not know what he faces. They can
not see the waste you have shown me. the People cast
down and broken in heart while all around them the
Wasichus crawl upon the land like ants upon a corpse.
Why have you shown me the horror of a time when
the Lakota are no longer the People but only men,
when the sacred ways have become forgotten and
all live half-lives without meaning? What shall I do?
You have shown me these things, Grandfathers, but I
am not strong enough, I am not worthy. Who would
lead in such a time? I am frightened but I must show
no fear, I am weak but I must seem strong. I must be
all-knowing when I know nothing. Like the powerless
frog, I must afright my enemies and embolden my
people with an empty roar. They lean upon me as an
old man upon a staff, but I am but a reed, trembling
and hollow. What must I do? Hey! Hey! Hey! Hey!

(Enter WITNAKE *and* GRUARD, *standing apart from* CRAZY
HORSE.*)*

WITNAKE: His spirit is greatly troubled with the
burdens of his people. He carries them all with him
into the other world. Take care you do not bring him
back too quickly. He may kill you for it.

GRUARD: I am beset by men with torments. Three Stars
wrestles in his mind with old enemies, too.

CRAZY HORSE: I see you, Yugata.

GRUARD: I see you, Tasunke Witco.

*(*GRUARD *extends his left arm to shake but* CRAZY HORSE
pointedly refuses it.)

CRAZY HORSE: I will not shake the hand of a Washichu.
You are a Washichu now aren't you, "Gruard"?

GRUARD: I am what I have always been—what you see.

CRAZY HORSE: I see a man who lived among the People then fled to the Wasichus when we took the path of war. I see a fool who knows the way of the Lakota but chooses to live in the service of an old man astride a mule.

GRUARD: Then you see me but dimly. I am a man who knows both peoples and seeks peace for all.

WITNAKE: (*Derisively*) Tell Crazy Horse of Three Stars and his plan for "peace".

GRUARD: I am sent to say he bids you return to the agency and the great chief Red Cloud and the others of your brethren who bide peacefully there. It is a safe place and secure and once there he promises you the manifold blessings of civilization.

CRAZY HORSE: These are not your words, Gruard.

GRUARD: It is a pretty speech I have by rote. I say it well.

WITNAKE: Tell us of the other offer, the one you make at the agency.

GRUARD: (*Pause*) He wants Lakota scouts. He offers a new rifle, ponies, a uniform if you wish, and an annuity for every man who volunteers and serves faithfully.

WITNAKE: An annuity?

GRUARD: A sum of money every year for the rest of your life.

WITNAKE: (*Laughs*) He is insane. You are led by this fool? What good is your money?

GRUARD: It has much use in the white world.

CRAZY HORSE: It has but one purpose for a Lakota. To buy the whisky that enslaves us. Is that what Three Stars offers us, Gruard? A chance to earn our own enslavement? You are fortunate that no one has killed you yet.

WITNAKE: He is not important enough. We could not count coup on a coward.

CRAZY HORSE: You are not a coward, are you, Gruard? You come among us still smelling of the soldier's tent. You know that many despise and some might slay you because your odor offends. And yet you came. You are not a coward. What are you?

GRUARD: I'm just a messenger.

CRAZY HORSE: Your work is perilous, but there is no honor in it. This Three Stars must hold strong magic to make you risk yourself this way. What is he like?

GRUARD: Crazy Horse is a great leader, a great warrior, a great chief...

WITNAKE: He is greater than Red Cloud. His valor shadows Spotted Tail.

GRUARD: ...but Three Stars, too, has proven himself in battle.

CRAZY HORSE: (*Proudly, angrily*) I have counted eighty-six coup! I have scalped Pawnee and Shoshone and I have killed a Crow and his wife and his child within his own tent. I have stolen thousands of horses and won battles against all my enemies.

GRUARD: General Crook has taken the lance from the hands of the Apache.

WITNAKE: What is an Apache?

GRUARD: A tribe from the arid South called Arizona. They live many days' ride from here in the desert.

WITNAKE: (*Sneers*) An Apache is not one of the People. What does it mean to take an Apache lance?

GRUARD: Many lives. It is Crook's great accomplishment.

CRAZY HORSE: I know nothing of what you call Apache. I am Lakota and Three Stars snaps at my heels all summer like an impudent dog. When I turn to face him he flees. Should I fear such a man?

GRUARD: As the wise man fears the wolf. He will hound you, and when you are weary, he will bite.

CRAZY HORSE: We have destroyed yellow haired Custer, why should we dread this tired old man?

GRUARD: Custer wanted just to kill you; Three Stars sees farther. He has not Custer's glory nor bluster, but this wise and reasoned old man would scare me far worse. He's got the devil's mind.

WITNAKE: He loses men in every skirmish! Soon there will be none left.

GRUARD: There are more Wasichu than a man can count in his lifetime.

WITNAKE: We will fight a lifetime and count the dead at its end. If there are so many Wasichu, then we must reclaim our arrows and use them twice. I hope they come to us as thick as buffalo that even a child can shoot and hit an enemy. Bring them in their masses, I have a son not yet with teeth, I will arm him and give him practice at a large target.

GRUARD: There are more of them than there are buffalo.

WITNAKE: There is no number greater than the buffalo! He is a liar and a fool to come here. No Lakota will ever serve as scout! Tell him, cousin.

CRAZY HORSE: I am no Wasichu. I do not set rules for others. Each man is free to be what he will.

WITNAKE: No Lakota will serve as scout! We have none so base. This request makes mockery of council.

CRAZY HORSE: Leave us awhile to speak alone, cousin.

WITNAKE: (*Saving face*) I need hear no more from this man. (*He exits.*)

GRUARD: If noise were courage Witnake would cause a bear to blanch with fear.

CRAZY HORSE: Do not reckon things too subtly. A man is often what he seems and he who bellows with courage can be brave.

GRUARD: He is a chief of his village and sees only as far as is given a man to see, but Crazy Horse is the chief of a nation and must envision the world across with the eyes of the eagle.

CRAZY HORSE: ...What you said of the Wasichus's numbers. Is it true? Can they be so vast?

GRUARD: They are as many as the locust in a swarm that blanks the sun.

CRAZY HORSE: ...Gruard, why do you do it? You have lived with the People, you have shared our triumphs, you have loved one of our women.... Why do you heed the soldiers? Did we mistreat you?

GRUARD: The People treated me well.

CRAZY HORSE: Do you have a complaint? Was there an injustice?

GRUARD: You are a just people.

CRAZY HORSE: Has someone stolen from you? Did another take your ponies? Your weapon?

GRUARD: I was treated with respect.

CRAZY HORSE: Did any judge you because of your color or your features?

GRUARD: I was judged only on my merit.

CRAZY HORSE: Then why do you help the soldiers against us?

GRUARD: Tasunke Witco, if your village was crossing a river and a great flood came and everyone was drowning, what would you do?

CRAZY HORSE: I would save my people.

GRUARD: You are one man, the flood is overwhelming, you can swim, the others can not. What would you do?

CRAZY HORSE: I would save my people, I have told you.

GRUARD: They will pull you under if you stay, you will drown with them.

CRAZY HORSE: (Shrugs) I will save them. What else can I do?

GRUARD: I would swim for shore. Most men would.

CRAZY HORSE: If you think that, you do not know the heart of the Lakotah.

GRUARD: No one knows the heart of another. We can only try to know our own. I see myself, I am the size of other men, I eat as they do, I drink as they do, I love the sun and dread the cold as they. Their stomachs are the same as mine, their eyes, their arms; shall I think their hearts so different? If others do not swim for shore, I must think they can not swim...or can not see the flood. I am not a saint. Like a hungry bird, I will turn to the parent that brings me food.

CRAZY HORSE: Your son is Lakotah.

GRUARD: My son is dead. He was slain by a Crow as he rode on a raid for horses—led by you.

CRAZY HORSE: I had forgotten.

GRUARD: Of course. He was only a boy of fourteen.

CRAZY HORSE: I have seen many die.

GRUARD: It was the raid when you killed the Crow named Many Knives. You gained much glory.

CRAZY HORSE: I had forgotten your son.

GRUARD: You were busy that day.

CRAZY HORSE: I have so many to remember. He died with honor. We mourn him still.

GRUARD: Some more than others.

CRAZY HORSE: It is not just to blame me for every death of every man on every raid.

GRUARD: No. It is not just.

CRAZY HORSE: It is a death with honor to fall against the Crow.

GRUARD: We raided the Crow to steal their pony herd. We had ponies enough, we didn't need the Crow's.

CRAZY HORSE: All ponies belong to the People.... And your woman...

GRUARD: Mikata lekta.

CRAZY HORSE: Yes. Lives she with you in a Wasichu wooden house?

GRUARD: The woman has died.

CRAZY HORSE: (*Covers his mouth and says*) Hush-sh. (*In ritual for the dead*) I knew not. Did she die of the Wasichu pox?

GRUARD: She passed with grief from the death of our boy, as some would have it, but I say it was the blade she drew across her throat that did her in. But then she was but a woman who valued the love of a child above a few ponies more or the glory of a scalp-lock to fringe a shirt. Perhaps I married ill—you knew her, Crazy Horse.

CRAZY HORSE: Not well.

GRUARD: No matter. She was a woman, quick to laugh, warm at night, with gentle hands and softer ways. A woman. Perhaps over-good at sorrow. She bore things ill. Thrice she carried my child and each try dropped it ere its time. And when at last she learned the birthing lesson and gave us our fourth alive and suckled him upon her breast and watched him grow and sent him off to war with a mother's plea for safety amidst the valor—why when he was felled and gave his hair to adorn a warrior's lodge, she was again ill equipped at bearing. She couldn't uphold his loss and so in excess of mourning killed herself... A woman.

CRAZY HORSE: And in death—how did you treat her?

GRUARD: Very like a corpse, not knowing other manners.

CRAZY HORSE: Did you put her in the ground like a Wasichu wife, food for worms and wolves? Or did you treat her like a Lakota that she may join her ancestors?

GRUARD: She is free to join whom she pleases, with my blessing, but most time she prefers to stay with me, out of old habit, for she visits me every night, her throat still a smile, our dead boy in her arms.

CRAZY HORSE: (*Hushing motions, sound*) Such things should not be spoken of.

GRUARD: You are right. Let us speak of war and peace and mighty deeds for women and children take no share in such manly things. What message shall I return to Three Stars?

CRAZY HORSE: Tell him he is a generous man and I would be shamed if I could not meet his offer with my own. I will give a fine pony and a buffalo robe to every soldier who comes to scout for us against the Wasichu.

GRUARD: He will not find the humor in your offer. The Wasichu do not know the Lakota sense of fun.

CRAZY HORSE: You are a dour people, Gruard. I have
seen Wasichus laugh only at drunken Lakotas. But tell
Three Stars to keep on my trail and I will show him
merriment without need of the burning cup... And look
to yourself, Yugata. You are confused and warring
within, and led by passions that spring not from honor.
You have tasted the last of our hospitality. Eat and
leave. If you come again, I do not know you. (*He exits.*)

GRUARD: You do not know me now. I am one man to
you, to Crook another, to each the man you most need
to see. I know you both—and you know me not all.
Call me two-faced? I would not be so impoverished. I
have a dozen faces if cause may need. Crook sees me
cunning and Crazy Horse weak while to the stripling
Clark I am a source of ribald fun, forever lewd and
leering. No matter. They are roles simple enough to
play and shall the need arise I will improvise another
mask. Men will continue to see me from the side and
none shall view me whole till I have completed my
purpose. I have lost two loves within a week to lay at
the feet of Crazy Horse, first son, then mother, quaffed
to slake the Lakota thirst for blood. If he deems death
such an honor I shall serve it up to him with joy. I shall
look to myself as you bid me, Crazy Horse, and I bid
you do the same. I curry Three Star's favor for a simple
cause. I do not chart the course of nations, I lack the
grandeur to decide the fate of peoples—and that fate
is sealed in any case. I wish but one thing from Crook
that I can not get myself. I will have the scalp of Crazy
Horse upon my lodge before the year is out.

(*Scene changes and* GRUARD *exits. There is a skirl of light
and sound, a mix of martial music and Indian war chant.*
CLARK *and* CROOK *enter.*)

CLARK: General, the Sioux set fire to the prairie!

CROOK: Withdraw to the river and let it pass.

CLARK: Shouldn't we attack, sir?

CROOK: These are his conditions. We will wait for ours.

(Shadows of several Indians mount the rise and wave and jeer at the SOLDIERS.*)*

CLARK: They're mocking us, sir!

CROOK: No, they bait us. Stand your ground.

CLARK: Can I send a detachment to deal with those few?

CROOK: Do you have a detachment you've marked for death? Stand your ground.

(Indians continue to taunt and jeer until CRAZY HORSE *recalls them with a gesture.)*

CLARK: The fire has stopped.

CROOK: There will be others. He's not trying to burn us out. he is destroying the pasture for our mounts.

*(*CRAZY HORSE, WITNAKE *and Indians exit.)*

CROOK: After them, Lieutenant. We will press them.

(Scene changes. CROOK, CLARK *cross stage then stop.)*

CLARK: We've lost the trail, sir.

CROOK: Find it.

CLARK: They've vanished.

CROOK: They can't have vanished!

(Enter GRUARD.*)*

GRUARD: They have split themselves, General. Each village will go on its own.

CLARK: Go where?

GRUARD: In summer they have but one pursuit, to find the buffalo. We can follow only one trail without splitting ourselves.

CROOK: Can you discern the trail of the village of Crazy Horse?

GRUARD: I can. His is a double village now; he travels with his cousin Witnake.

CROOK: We will follow Crazy Horse.

CLARK: One of the other villages might be easier to subdue.

CROOK: We will follow the leader.

(Scene changes, CRAZY HORSE *and* WITNAKE *enter on one side of stage,* CROOK, CLARK *and* GRUARD *take positions on the other side. A battle ensues.)*

CLARK: We have their camp!

CROOK: Attack.

*(*CRAZY HORSE *and* WITNAKE *turn, taken by surprise)*

WITNAKE: The soldiers!

(Bugle sounds the attack.)

WITNAKE: We're surrounded!

CLARK: They're on the run! We have them, General!

CROOK: Press them.

WITNAKE: The soldiers have taken our ponies!

CROOK: Press them.

WITNAKE: They're into the camp!

CRAZY HORSE: *(Piercing war cry)* It's a good day to fight and a good day to die! Lakotah, follow me!

*(*WITNAKE *and Indians take heart and charge after* CRAZY HORSE, *sounding their cries. The battle is turned.)*

CLARK: They've recaptured their horses!

CROOK: Press them.

CLARK: They're attacking our own horses...they've got our herd! ...Fall back, men! Fall back!

WITNAKE: (*Triumphantly*) They're running off! We have defeated them!

(CRAZY HORSE *stands alone atop the rise, brandishing a soldier's bloody cap as a trophy over his head. He looks directly at* CROOK, *who looks back up at him. There is a moment of understanding between the two generals.* CRAZY HORSE *unleashes a bloodcurdling yell of triumph, then exits along with the Indians.*)

CROOK: (*To* CRAZY HORSE's *back*) It is still summer.

CLARK: General, they took our horses.

CROOK: We will pursue them.

CLARK: We lost ten men, sir.

CROOK: And the Sioux?

CLARK: Only one that I know of, and they took the body with them.

CROOK: We will press them.

CLARK: They took the horses, sir.

CROOK: (*Angrily*) Then we will march! Send to Fort Fetterman for more horses and more men. They can meet us at the Powder River. We must not lose touch with him.

CLARK: Every time we touch him, he bites us.

CROOK: Would you fight this campaign from your bed? Press them.

CLARK: We have pursued them all summer, the men are exhausted, the horses are gone, our supplies are low...

CROOK: Our day will come and we must go forward to meet it. If we rest, he rests, and when he does he grows stronger.

CLARK: He grows stronger with our horses and our supplies whenever we meet. He dines on us.

CROOK: A man can die from overeating; we will stay lean. He is in his strength in the summer, but we must not allow him to rest. When winter comes he will be weakened. Gather the men, give them their duties, prepare to march. We press them.

CLARK: And what of our dead?

CROOK: We will mourn en route. Bury them together by the river bank. We will march over the grave as we leave so the Sioux can not find and defile our fallen. Hurry now while his track is still warm. One thing is certain about a hot trail, you'll find Indians on it if you go far enough, and you'll find them nowhere else.

(Scene changes to Indian camp, a great bonfire rages. WITNAKE *and* CRAZY HORSE *enter.)*

WITNAKE: *(Exultantly)* Two Crow scouts fell within our hands like bursting plums in Three Star's bluest coat and hats. They being infrequent guests we made to bid them welcome but one chose to die first. For the second we cut the tendons of wrists and feet and held him deep within the consuming blaze by poles of pine. I lofted my infant son upon my shoulders that he might see a Crow die well.

CRAZY HORSE: Any Crow death is well done.... What of the soldiers?

WITNAKE: They lie a day behind, encircled and afraid. Let us turn and crush them.

CRAZY HORSE: They attack poorly but defend well. The cost would be too high.

WITNAKE: Our triumphs are without end. We scatter the blue coats by waving our arms as a man may afright a timorous dog. Three Stars loses five men to one of ours. With such favoring odds let us stake all and be done with this nuisance.

CRAZY HORSE: Such odds do not favor us. My warriors are of my village, I have supped and fought and wept with each. Each death is my diminishment, each fallen tears from me a portion of my past, my life, my memory. None can be replaced. Three Stars pays no such price for battle. He hears no widow's cries. He fights in the company of strangers and knows not the men who die for him. They come to serve from distant lodges and do not weigh upon his soul when they are gone.

WITNAKE: Let me ride for the other villages. Each will send its bravest at your call, each will gladly share the loss.

CRAZY HORSE: They must hunt, as must we all. We need the summer hide of the young cows lest our lodge skins rot in winter.

WITNAKE: The squaws complain we have no time to dry the meat, scurrying as we are to avoid the soldiers' bite. Let us kill the dog that hounds us.

CRAZY HORSE: If we turn, he turns, if we charge he falls back, if we flee, he pursues. We have not the time to spare. The buffalo moves on and so must we. Winter will come though Three Stars follows or no.

WITNAKE: We have survived bad winters before—but not in flight.

CRAZY HORSE: We must hunt.

WITNAKE: If we had not split our bands we could have turned and squashed Three Stars with the effort of a morning.

CRAZY HORSE: Whom could I stop? I am chief for war, I tell no others when or where to hunt. By what authority could I stop the least of them from tending to his people? I can not stop you.

WITNAKE: Me? You have no need to stop me.

CRAZY HORSE: You will remove with your own village when winter comes.

WITNAKE: We will need to separate for the forage only. I am with you always in spirit. You have all I own for the asking, nay, simply by desiring. My very life is yours if you will but command it...I know you would do the same for me.

CRAZY HORSE: I am a chief, as are you. I can not hazard my life as a marker in a game, nor offer it to another as a sign of affection. It belongs not to me, but to my people.

WITNAKE: You are too harsh with me, cousin. I spoke with sincerity but lightly. I am as constant in my duty as any man.

CRAZY HORSE: Duty is like the fox's fur, it changes color with the season and is constant only in its purpose.

WITNAKE: Though it mask itself with the mottle of the young fawn I shall always recognize my duty to you.

CRAZY HORSE: Your duty is not to me, but to the people.

WITNAKE: You are the soul of the people.

CRAZY HORSE: (*Pause; agreeing*) I have been given the vision.

WITNAKE: Look, cousin, the scouts return with sign of the herd. We must go.

(CRAZY HORSE *stands for a moment, looking in direction of* CROOK's *camp.*)

WITNAKE: What keeps you?

CRAZY HORSE: There is no smoke from Three Stars' camp. They eat and sleep without fire.

WITNAKE: From fear of us.

CRAZY HORSE: The nights grow colder.

WITNAKE: The winter will crush him.

CRAZY HORSE: Outnumbered, outfought, with no hope of scalps, and yet he endures. In such a position any man would withdraw and seek the comfort of his lodge. Why does he persist?

WITNAKE: I do not understand the Wasichu.

CRAZY HORSE: To bend us to his will. (*Pause*) How strange a purpose. ...Come, the buffalo await.

(CRAZY HORSE *and* WITNAKE *exit. Scene changes to Army camp,* CROOK *is reading.* CLARK *enters.*)

CLARK: You requested a report on our status, sir.

CROOK: I would hear your opinion of it.

CLARK: Sir, the men are suffering badly. We have cases of neuralgia, rheumatism, dysentery, malaria. Trooper Sandstrom is violently insane and needs to be restrained...Lieutenant Van Lewyk's arm is shattered by a bullet and must come off.... We haven't eaten properly in weeks, we haven't had a change of clothes in a month.... We've lost over a hundred lives in these endless skirmishes.... We are in bad shape, sir. If there is another opinion, I would like to hear it.

CROOK: And the Sioux? How do they fare?

CLARK: The Sioux? I think we have somewhat annoyed them.... Sorry, sir. I don't know how they fare.

CROOK: If we return to the fort, we will have lost the advantage for which our men have suffered and died.

CLARK: Advantage? What advantage? Whenever we engage with Crazy Horse we lose men!

CROOK: And he loses time from the hunt. He is not a farmer, Clark. He does not set up grain for the winter, he does not can or pickle excess food. He has but one crop. When the snows come he lives off dried buffalo meat and wraps himself in buffalo robes and dresses himself in its skins. He burns buffalo fat in his fires and can not winter in this harsh land without fresh hides of the buffalo cow to make his lodges. If he has no buffalo he must eat his horses, and a Sioux afoot is not a Sioux. They are brave and bold warriors, Lieutenant, but they have grown used to property. They can not withstand its loss. They will not suffer like the Apache who had nothing to begin with. The Sioux is shackled to nature, he has no dominion over it as does the simplest farmer. He does not understand war of economy. He excels at battle. He can HIT! (*He grips* CLARK's *arm, slaps his hand violently.*) But he can not do THIS.

(CROOK *squeezes* CLARK's *hand, applying ever increasing pressure until* CLARK *cries out in pain.*)

CROOK: You withstood the strike easily enough.

(GRUARD *enters.*)

GRUARD: General, they move again.

CROOK: Towards the agency?

GRUARD: West, after the herd.

CROOK: They follow their harvest, Lieutenant. Prepare the men, we will march within the hour.

(CROOK, CLARK *and* GRUARD *exit. Scene changes, autumn comes amid wind and swirling leaves. There is a brief skirmish between Indians and* SOLDIERS, *a brief burst of their music. Enter* CLARK *and* GRUARD.)

CLARK: (*Upset*) And after the skirmish the Crow scouts found a Sioux warrior who had been blinded in the fight. The warrior heard them and thought they were his own people and he cried out for water...They cut him limb from limb and ripped off his scalp; laughing.

GRUARD: (*Shrugs*) It was coup for them. They have destroyed an enemy. One will proudly show the warrior's scalp on his lance.

CLARK: Proudly?

GRUARD: They do not have medals to pin upon their coats.

CLARK: What honor is it to sport scalps from the fallen blind?

GRUARD: There are taverns in Deadwood where Lakotah hair hangs above the bar.

CLARK: The random act of a few desperate men, not a society's way of life!

GRUARD: Do you ask me to defend it? They live for battle, they war with each other as they breathe. I have known them to ride eight hundred miles to find a fight and kill a foe. The Lakota gnaw upon their neighbors and given time will consume them all. They slay the Crow, the Shoshone, the Pawnee, the Cree, the Nez Perce and half a dozen more and gladly give up their youth in this pursuit. They have never known peace, they do not seek it, it does not suit their purpose. There are villages within this tribe where the women outnumber the men by three to one, so heavy is the toll they pay for their lust for blood.

CLARK: I do not understand why Crook admires the Indians so. He doesn't approve of what they do, but he speaks so highly of them.

GRUARD: What Crook admires is all the traits he wants to see that mirror the best of his own. What he doesn't like he wants to alter. You might teach a bear to use a knife and fork—but he's no longer any use as a bear, and you still don't invite him in for supper. (*Exits*)

CLARK: How is it all men speak with such definity save me? Crook finds a pattern in this maelstrom that to mine eyes is but screaming and grown men's tears. Our leader wars with such assurance, wielding convictions as both blade and shield, while to those of us who only serve and face where we are turned, there is no surety but fear...I am so afraid. I am no soldier born, I did mistake my call, I want no portion of this pain nor terror. They are a fiercesome enemy and my heart does quail again and again and I would hide myself within the keep of Pennsylvania's verdant hills. What holds me here, what keeps me? ...A strange regard for those with whom I serve. Slum-bred Irishmen and rawboned Dutch who grew to manhood without shoes and could no nearer read from Crook's great books than Egypt's tombs—and yet in the fury of the fight I would not let these comrades down. Most odd. I do not flee for love of men I do not like.... But these are the thoughts of solitude. The vise of cowardice grips most strong when I'm alone. I must join the men that we can draw courage from one another.

(CLARK *exits. Scene changes.* CRAZY HORSE *is in the grip of his dream. He rises from a lake and seems to float above the ground. Bullets and arrows and the sounds of battle are all around him but they all fall away without touching him. a violent storm breaks out with wind and rain and lighting and thunder but he passes through, unharmed. His own people surround him and clutch at him and try to hold him back. He struggles to get through them but they cling to him. The dream turns from one of triumph to a nightmare. He can not pull free from his people. They pin his arms behind him. He strains to be free but can not break their grip. He opens his mouth to cry out and the chilling shriek of an eagle emerges. He wakes. Greatly shaken, as* WITNAKE *enters.*)

CRAZY HORSE: (*Still in grip of dream*) Release me! Let me go!

WITNAKE: Release you? I have no hold on you.

CRAZY HORSE: What do you say?

(WITNAKE *puts a hand on* CRAZY HORSE's *shoulder.)*

WITNAKE: I am Witnake, you know me. There is no harm here.

CRAZY HORSE: I heard you sound the alarm.

WITNAKE: No. All is well.

CRAZY HORSE: Why do you press on me so? Stand away.

WITNAKE: *(Steps back)* What do you seek?

(CRAZY HORSE *scans the area.)*

CRAZY HORSE: The people. Where have they all so swiftly gone?

WITNAKE: There are none here...Your lodge is dark, smoke forms shapes against the walls...

CRAZY HORSE: Why do I dread their embrace in one world and think only of them in the other? ...I shall not abandon them, Witnake.

WITNAKE: None has ever thought...

CRAZY HORSE: I am their hope. I am their light now that the darkness falls upon us. Without me they will be lost.

WITNAKE: You light us as the sun...

CRAZY HORSE: Not the sun! Do not flatter me, I do not seek flattery. I am but a torch in the vastness of the night but the People must find their way by my light, I am the only torch left. I will not be extinguished by the storm of the white man. Do you know this, Witnake?

I shall not abandon the People, I shall not surrender them to the white man's burning cup. Do you know this?

WITNAKE: We all know this.

CRAZY HORSE: I will cut off my left arm before I ever clasp the hand of the white man. Do you know this?

WITNAKE: But why trouble your thoughts with surrender? We dine upon the soldiers as ripe berries, plucking now a horse, now a weapon as we will.

CRAZY HORSE: A warrior does not live on berries. Where is Three Stars?

WITNAKE: Somewhere in our dust, crouched in the shelter of his hole. He is a beaten dog who trails behind the camp.

CRAZY HORSE: A man is not a dog, he is not so surely subdued. You may beat your woman as soundly as you thrash a dog and have no fear of reprisal—until you sleep. A man is dangerous until he's dead.... (*Gazes into distance*) Is not our land beautiful?

WITNAKE: It is.

CRAZY HORSE: Has not the Great Spirit given us the best of all lands?

WITNAKE: He favors us above all others. It is natural that he should, for surely we are the most devout and deserving... But why does He suffer the Wasichus to take it from us?

CRAZY HORSE: It is a test and a trial. Those who have been given much in plenty must bear much in adversity. We will be equal to the test as long as we remain loyal to the old ways. Our strength is in our faith, Witnake, and the Powers will never abandon us as long as we are true to them.

WITNAKE: I would demonstrate our faith by wiping Three Stars off the land. The Spirits cherish a display of courage.

CRAZY HORSE: They cherish wisdom more. You need not tutor me on the Great Spirit unless your connection is more intimate than my own.

WITNAKE: I meant no...

CRAZY HORSE: Have you been given a vision?

WITNAKE: No.

CRAZY HORSE: Then I shall cling to mine as true... Why have you come?

WITNAKE: The beaver's pelt is thick this year. It will be a hard winter. Together our villages are too large to find good forage for all. I am taking my village south towards the mouth of the Tongue, I know good pasture there.

CRAZY HORSE: Yes, it is a good plan.

WITNAKE: If Three Stars threatens, you can send for me. My village is yours to command, always.

CRAZY HORSE: I am no blue coat, I can command no one. I have no power over any but my wives. You must do as you see right.

WITNAKE: (Pause) We will move to the Tongue.

(WITNAKE and CRAZY HORSE shake hands, clasping left arms.)

WITNAKE: Your village is as my village, your sorrows bring forth my grief.

CRAZY HORSE: I will move East towards the Powder and winter with the bluffs to our back.

WITNAKE: Can you give me nothing, cousin?

CRAZY HORSE: What do you wish?

WITNAKE: I offer you my allegiance, my people, my own life. It is an offer grown stale from repetition. Like a dish not to your appetite you finger it and pass it back. Will you have none of my devotion? Is it such an unworthy gift?

CRAZY HORSE: I wish no offense, cousin. I am proferred many gifts and many seek my favor. To prefer one is to scorn the multitude but to accept is to exhaust my charity. If a man gives me a gift I must return in kind or seem ungrateful but there are so many who would present me things that I should soon be beggared by such bounty.

WITNAKE: This is cold, cousin. I have not left a pony outside your lodge that needs repayment, I offer you my love.

CRAZY HORSE: (*Wearily*) I have so many to love. My warmth is for the People, I can not spare it singly...but I thank you, Witnake. Let that serve that there may be peace between us. (*He exits.*)

WITNAKE: Perhaps it is that greatness is best perceived from a distance. A mountain too close is but stone. Staring inward on great visions the great may appear to regard only themselves. But it is not so. It can not be so for without great leaders we would be left to divine the true path for ourselves...I will to my lodge and take my infant son into my arms and let his laughter warm me. In the innocence of youth, he takes me for great.

(*Exit* WITNAKE; *enter* GRUARD, CROOK)

GRUARD: They have split the village. One trail runs south and one east.

CROOK: Which is Crazy Horse?

GRUARD: The paths are of equal size.

CROOK: Chose.

GRUARD: I know not.

CROOK: Then I shall chose. We follow the trail heading south.

GRUARD: Towards the Tongue.

CROOK: If I chose correctly, towards the heart.

(Snow begins to fall then builds into a blizzard as all exit. The wind howls. A small fire glows. CLARK *enters to join* GRUARD *who is seated by the fire. Both wear heavy clothing.)*

CLARK: General Crook shelters in that beaver lodge where Gibbon's Rome declines at noon by candlelight.

GRUARD: Does that not discommode the beavers? I have seen the book. It is a lengthy yarn to spin a rodent.

CLARK: It is a wonderful book. *(Pause)* I have not had the pleasure to read it myself.

(Wind howls)

CLARK: I have never seen such a winter.

GRUARD: It is the unrestricted wind.

CLARK: The men are suffering badly. Trooper Simmons even has frostbite of his member.

GRUARD: Simmons will learn to piss downwind. It is remarkable careless to leave such a property so long exposed. It is not a toe, one has no spare.

(Enter CROOK.*)*

CLARK: *(Rising)* I thought you were reading, sir.

CROOK: It is at times a lonely distraction...I have seen that the men have what little comfort there is.

*(*CROOK *motions* CLARK *to sit. Awkward pause)*

CROOK: You graduated from the Academy, did you, Clark?

CLARK: Yes, sir. Class of '73.

CROOK: The texts can not prepare one for the cold, nor the mud of spring.

CLARK: No, sir... Nor the sight of dying men.

CROOK: No... It has little to do with books... How does he fare now, Gruard; the Lakota?

GRUARD: (*Shrugs*) He's cold. His nostrils freeze. His breath turns white.

CLARK: He must have special ways to warm in such a clime.

GRUARD: He endures. That is his great secret. He endures.

CROOK: He has one advantage for suffering—he has not known otherwise.... When I was a lad in Ohio, I saw my first Indian in the village square, drunk and puking while the whites taunted him with promise of more liquor if he would dance. He danced, and I laughed, and my father yanked me from there and boxed my ears. "That is no longer an Indian." he said. "And there is nothing funny there."

GRUARD: The first Indian I saw was a woman. She prepared a meal and regarded me not at all though I must have looked as strange to her as she to me... Lacking her simple courtesy I gaped awhile—and found her lovely. (*Pause*) I was younger then, as was the world.

CLARK: Do you miss living with them, Gruard?

GRUARD: I miss those I miss. They are but human, after all, and can annoy and comfort in a hundred different ways. We have the same percent of fools and friends within this army camp—though no women, which does decrease the comfort some.

CLARK: (*Laughs*) The topic is always much the same with you.

GRUARD: I was never so careless as Trooper Simmons.

CLARK: (*To* CROOK) By your leave, I must check the pickets.

CROOK: Tend your duties, son.

CLARK: ...If you like, we can speak more when I return.

(CROOK *nods,* CLARK *exits. Wind howls.*)

CROOK: It is an awful place to live and seems not worth the dying for.

GRUARD: I have yet to find what is.

CROOK: Keep searching, Gruard. It would be a sad thing to die for naught.

GRUARD: Sad, perhaps, but I leave none to feel the sorrow. (*Stands*)

CROOK: Do not leave on my account.

GRUARD: I must see to the scouts...I can send someone to keep you company.

CROOK: Do not. My presence makes men too conscientious of their duties. Let them rest.

(*Exit* GRUARD. CROOK *sits alone awhile with the wind and the cold. Time passes.* CLARK *enters.*)

CLARK: General! McKenzie has struck their village! We have taken them completely by surprise!

CROOK: Is there resistance?

CLARK: We have captured the women and children!

CROOK: What of the men?

CLARK: The warriors occupy the rocks above us but they are without horse and few weapons! It is a total victory, sir!

CROOK: Not while they still resist. Offer them surrender.

CLARK: Gruard is talking to them but they remain defiant. It is no matter, sir. We hit them so fast the bucks fled to the rocks without their robes or blankets. We have but to hold them there and we'll freeze them out!

CROOK: Is Crazy Horse among them?

CLARK: (*Pause*) This is not his village. It's under a chief called Witnake.

CROOK: Damn! I am plagued by quicksilver.

CLARK: What of the captives?

CROOK: They are free to return to the agency.

CLARK: What shall we do with their lodges?

CROOK: Burn them.

(*The women wail.*)

CLARK: Sir...without shelter, in this weather...

CROOK: Burn the lodges, the food, the robes and blankets, the cooking pots, the weapons. Make a blaze bright enough for Crazy Horse to see be he leagues away.

(*The women set up a great cry.* WITNAKE *stands on the rise, sees what is happening.*)

WITNAKE: My son!

(*All exit as the stage is consumed in the sight and sound of flames. Scene changes to* CRAZY HORSE's *lodge.* WITNAKE *enters, freezing and exhausted.*)

CRAZY HORSE: What do you ask of me?

WITNAKE: Our women and old folk are walking towards the Red Cloud agency. They have killed their few ponies so that the old people can warm their feet and hands in the steaming entrails of the animals.

CRAZY HORSE: We are slaughtering our own ponies. Crook has driven us across the lands we burned last summer; there is no fodder for the ponies and they die.

WITNAKE: Our women must eat, they carry nothing with them...

CRAZY HORSE: The soldiers gave us no pause to dry our meat. It has rotted and we live off rabbits and our dogs.

WITNAKE: At least blankets, robes, clothing...

CRAZY HORSE: We had no time to replace the skins of our lodges, these are worn thin and crack and the wind screams through them. We awake with snow on our bodies.

WITNAKE: You must give us something!

CRAZY HORSE: I have nothing to give. We have not enough for ourselves.

WITNAKE: If you do not share with us, my village will die!

CRAZY HORSE: If I share with you, both our villages will die.

WITNAKE: Cousin, my child is among the helpless.

CRAZY HORSE: Do you think there are no children in my village? Shall I doom them that your son may live?

WITNAKE: Then I will take from the Wasichus.

CRAZY HORSE: If you take from the soldiers you may live—but your children's children will wither at birth. The Lakotah people will sing a death chant if you take from the Wasichu.

WITNAKE: (Pause) I can not let my people die. There is no honor in freezing and starvation.

CRAZY HORSE: Honor is living like a Lakotah—and dying like one when the time comes.

WITNAKE: I will not condemn my innocent son to death while I have the means to save him!

CRAZY HORSE: You will do as you must. As do I.

(WITNAKE *exits.* CRAZY HORSE, *atop the rise, is enveloped in a blizzard. He lifts his head to the heavens and begins to chant. we hear Indian women, suffering and wailing.* CLARK *and* CROOK *enter, survey the women)*

CLARK: Sir...if we could help them...

CROOK: It is in the power of their warriors to help them. Let them decide.

(GRUARD *enters with* WITNAKE.)

GRUARD: General, this is Witnake. He's the chief of the village you just destroyed. I know this man.

(WITNAKE *bows his head.*)

CROOK: I have no need for obeisance. Tell him I am a servant of my government and I am here to help him and his people.

GRUARD: I imagine he knows that by now.

CLARK: Translate, Gruard, without interpolation.

(GRUARD *turns to* WITNAKE. *They speak in English but for the moment it is clear that* CROOK *and* CLARK *do not understand them.*)

WITNAKE: What has he said?

GRUARD: You're not so proud, now my friend.

WITNAKE: I can still put a blade in your heart.

(WITNAKE *touches his knife.* CLARK *springs to defend* CROOK, *thinking the hostility is aimed at him.*)

CLARK: Guard!

(SOLDIER *with rifle runs on, points it at* WITNAKE *who is first defiant of guard, too, then slowly calms down.*)

CROOK: Let your heart be at ease. You have nothing to fear from us if you return to the agency and cease your hostilities.... Tell him, Gruard.

WITNAKE: I am a war chief, I am a member of the eagle Shirt Society, I have counted many coups, seven of your own soldiers. I will not be insulted by a traitor like Gruard.

CROOK: What does he say?

GRUARD: Ceremony. He tells you he's a fine fellow and you're lucky to have him standing before you, shivering like a new born calf.

CROOK: Render me the words, Gruard. I'll settle on the substance. Tell him I'm honored to have him in my camp and ask how I may serve him.

GRUARD: (*To* WITNAKE) What do you want?

WITNAKE: Food for my people, clothing, shelter. We can not survive the winter!

GRUARD: A day ago you wanted his scalp and now you ask his help. Why should he offer you so much as the scrapings of his food bowl?

CROOK: What does he say?

WITNAKE: I offer my friendship.

GRUARD: Friendship of the mighty is a powerful thing—from the defeated it is a paltry gift.

CROOK: What does he say!

GRUARD: You ask much of Three Stars. What do you give in return?

(*Women wail in suffering.*)

WITNAKE: (*Pause*) I will scout for him.

GRUARD: (*Triumphantly; to* CROOK) He'll help you catch Crazy Horse.

CROOK: Amen!

(CRAZY HORSE, *atop the rise, emits a shattering wail of sorrow which becomes the shriek of the eagle as it flies overhead, then vanishes.)*

(Black out)

END OF ACT ONE

ACT TWO

(At rise, the Indian music is funereal. CRAZY HORSE *slowly mounts the rise as a blizzard falls. He carries a buffalo robe on his bare shoulders but lets it fall to the ground.)*

CRAZY HORSE: Hey! Hey! Hey! Hey! Grandfather, behold me! The Great Circle is broken and our lives fall awry. The Wasichu swarm across the land like maggots on a bone while Lakotah wither and die. Brave men who once would welcome a lance to their entrails to save the People now sell their daughters to white men for another taste of the burning cup that mocks their real courage with a spineless choler spending itself in boastful roar and vomit.

Even fruitful nature has fallen sere and barren before the Lakotah hand. The grasses cringe beneath the snow, the great four-leggeds have returned to the earth. My people starve. Great Powers, what is needed to restore the balance? I have fasted, I have done the dance of the sun; I have cleansed and purified myself and sought the vision time and again. I live only for my people, I ask nothing for myself. I am nothing before you. If a dog lift his leg against my lodge, I do not see it. What must I do?

(Enter WITNAKE *and* GRUARD. WITNAKE *wears an Army coat with Indian leggings)*

CRAZY HORSE: And the eaters of carrion fold their wings and advance.

WITNAKE: We come in peace.

CRAZY HORSE: So, Witnake, you are now a man of the future. Like your dress, no longer Lakotah but not quite Wasichu. A beast of two parts but no heart.

WITNAKE: It is but a coat. I can remove it.

CRAZY HORSE: It fits you well. A practical garment, I see, with pockets and buttons. Practical garb for a most practical man.

WITNAKE: It is well to dress against the cold, all wise men do it.

CRAZY HORSE: If I wear bear skin or eagle feather, it is to gain their strength and wisdom. What virtue do you seek from Wasichu cloth?

GRUARD: I speak to you for Three Stars who is your friend.

CRAZY HORSE: I have never met him but I am glad to hear he is my friend. I have been much in need of friends lately.

GRUARD: General Crook offers you surrender.

CRAZY HORSE: He is a generous man. Tell him I offer him the same, it would be discourteous to offer less.

WITNAKE: : The soldiers are only a mile from your village.

CRAZY HORSE: And I a mile from them.

GRUARD: We have with us more than a thousand Lakotah scouts, armed and eager to battle your village.

CRAZY HORSE: (Stunned) A thousand? It can not be.

WITNAKE: It is true. All from my village and the rest from the agency when they heard you would not feed us.

CRAZY HORSE: I could not feed you.

GRUARD: Fresh warriors, their bellies full. Crook
has promised each horses and an annuity if he fight
bravely.

CRAZY HORSE: They will not fight their brothers! We
are not Crow! We are all Lakotah!

GRUARD: They are Minniconjou, Brule, Hunkpapa. You
are Oglala, not their brothers. Cousins, perhaps. Many
blame the Oglala for the government's wrath.

WITNAKE: They urge you to come to the agency. Red
Cloud and Spotted Tail send word for you to return.
Your people would welcome you home, we do not
wish to fight you.

GRUARD: But they will. Crook will send them in
advance of the soldiers. Many are young, they would
stand tall as giants with a coup against the great Crazy
Horse.

WITNAKE: We beg you to come home.

CRAZY HORSE: Home? Again you call it home? This is
home. Does not the wind blow here? Does not the rain
fall? Do not the buffalo and elk pass this valley? Or
that? Or that?
  I am a Lakotah. Home is where I raise my lodge.

(Keening of women is loud and close. WITNAKE *stares in
their direction.)*

WITNAKE: Another child has died. Whose child is this?

CRAZY HORSE: If he is a Lakotah, he is mine.

WITNAKE: *(Of the child)* Let there be no more of this!

CRAZY HORSE: I do not cause it.

WITNAKE: You do not stop it. A father may die for his
children, he does not allow them to die for him.

CRAZY HORSE: ...I will meet with Three Stars.

GRUARD: *(Pause)* There will be some slight ceremony.

WITNAKE: What ceremony?

GRUARD: Nothing grand, Crook is a simple man. You will smoke a pipe, you will exchange small gifts, of course.

CRAZY HORSE: That is proper. I will give him a purse with fine bead work.

GRUARD: Three Stars would like your rifle and bow.... They make a fitting gift.

CRAZY HORSE: (*Pause*) It is a plain bow, an ordinary rifle, he has many such. The purse has designs of great artistry.

GRUARD: Three Stars has plain tastes, he would cherish a weapon from Tsunke Witco.

(CRAZY HORSE *unsheaths his knife and holds it to* GRUARD's *throat.*)

CRAZY HORSE: Do not speak my true name! You have no right to it! It sounds a curse on your traitorous tongue.

GRUARD: I apologize to Crazy Horse.

CRAZY HORSE: I must purify the taint of your bad medicine in the sweat lodge.

GRUARD: It was a mistake! I am most sorry.

(CRAZY HORSE *releases* GRUARD, *sheathes the knife.*)

CRAZY HORSE: (*Pause*) If he desires them, I shall make this gift to Three Stars.

GRUARD: ...and you must shake hands.

WITNAKE: No!

GRUARD: As ceremony.

WITNAKE: This is Crazy Horse! He will never shake the hand of a white man.

GRUARD: It is a small courtesy. Crook desires it.

CRAZY HORSE: I can not. It goes against a sacred vow.
Three Stars will understand the sanctity of a vow.

GRUARD: It is an insult not to shake his hand.

WITNAKE: It is more than a vow. Crazy Horse has
promised us.

GRUARD: A promise made in different times.

WITNAKE: I say he must not shake. I and one thousand
scouts say he must not. He will meet with Three Stars,
he will make him a gift of his weapons and smoke the
pipe. He will not shake hands.

CRAZY HORSE: You say this, who come to fight against
me?

WITNAKE: I am not a holy man, I am not a great one,
I do what I must for my children and the helpless to
survive. But you are our pride. You must not bow.

CRAZY HORSE: I am but a man, Witnake.

WITNAKE: No, you have chosen to be otherwise. We
have believed you. You can not change now.

(WITNAKE, CRAZY HORSE *exit*, GRUARD *joins* CLARK *and*
CROOK *who enter.* CLARK *carries uniform coat, sword, sash,
etc, for* CROOK.)

CLARK: Wear this, sir. The Indians are much impressed
by finery.

CROOK: Custer's stars and furbelows availed him little
enough. Let Crazy Horse be impressed by his hunger.
And if that fail, we have two thousand troops with
carbines.

(GRUARD *crosses to* CROOK.)

GRUARD: Ceremony is important to these people,
General. They esteem the doing of a thing as grand as
the thing itself.

CROOK: The act of surrender is convincing enough, let us do it and be done.

GRUARD: For the native mind, the joy is in the steps and not the music.

CLARK: We don't want to insult them, sir. Let them think they have lost to a mighty force.

CROOK: I would not give offense. Very well, teach me sweet courtesy, but in haste. I wish to have this matter settled. Our real work with the Sioux is yet to come.

GRUARD: Tis custom to trade small gifts at such a time. He would value something of your own, a bit of cloth that you have warn, your hat perhaps. Take it from your head and fix it firmly on his own. He will take it as a friendly gesture.

CLARK: An honor, I'd say.

GRUARD: Indeed. The man will be proud to wear it like his own.

CROOK: Very well. Yes, yes, say on.

GRUARD: He'll make a talk, you orate some...something of the flowery kind with figures of speech and so forth, they're partial to that.

CROOK: I will speak to them of truth.

GRUARD: They're bound to like that.

CROOK: And I will paint for them a picture of the future that can be theirs.

CLARK: That'll be popular, sir.

GRUARD: The Indian's got a rather limited notion of the future, General. He's not what you call progressive. His idea of a great tomorrow is more of the same he's got today. His only notion of change is the turning of the seasons.

CROOK: Then I will inform him of the way the world turns. Great things await the Sioux if they will but step forward to meet them. Come. I, for one, am eager.

(CROOK *crosses towards exit,* GRUARD, CLARK *follow.*)

GRUARD: There's one thing of great importance, general. When you're finished with your palaver, shake his hand. You're the conqueror, so don't wait on him, just thrust out your left arm and shake his.

(*They exit.* CRAZY HORSE *enters on rise. Indians present him with war bonnet, elaborately beaded robes, etc. he puts them all aside, removes his buffalo robe and the stone he wears on a thong under his armpit, and goes to meet* CROOK *simply dressed. He stands.*)

(*On the rise, waiting for* CROOK, *martial music is heard.* WITNAKE *enters and stands, watching* CRAZY HORSE.)

(CROOK, CLARK, GRUARD *enter with ceremony.* CROOK *wears a hat and the finery.* CLARK *is also dressed formally and wears a white hat.*)

CRAZY HORSE: I see you, Three Stars.

CROOK: I see you, Crazy Horse.

(CRAZY HORSE *holds his higher position for a moment, then descends to* CROOK *and gives him his rifle and bow.*)

CRAZY HORSE: I present you a gift.

CROOK: I am honored...I have a gift for you.

(CROOK *puts his hat on* CRAZY HORSE's *head.* CRAZY HORSE *Is startled and he stiffens. The Indians are tense.*)

CRAZY HORSE: Three Stars does me great honor. But it does not fit. I shall be proud to hang it in my lodge. (*He removes the hat.*)

GRUARD: It can be made to fit.

CRAZY HORSE: It is too valuable to wear, my people would think me boastful if I dressed myself like the great Three Stars.

CROOK: It is good that you have come in. You and your people are always in danger when you are off the agency. We want your families to be safe and well cared for.

CRAZY HORSE: It is as you say: we are always in danger out there. But I am told you are the one who can stop the danger. I am told you know how the world must be, that we have struggled for our lifetimes and do not know what you know about how to avoid danger or how to get food or how to stay dry in a storm. I am told your knowledge is so vast that you must be the one who makes the green pastures, who sends the rain, who commands the wind. For it is you who determines who may eat—and whether they deserve to have food at all. Prior to your coming, in our ignorance we ate when we were hungry and shared our food with all but you know better and you have said that only those who live on the agency may eat. It seems you are right for those with you are as fat as soldiers while my village has chewed their own mocassins in the winter and our skin hangs loose upon our bones. Since you are the one who controls the food I shall watch with awe as you bring forth fruit upon the trees in springtime.

CLARK: This is arrogance!

CROOK: Let it pass.

CRAZY HORSE: There are many men in the world who are big chiefs and command many people, but Three Stars, I think, is the greatest of them all. You want to be our father and to instruct us as your children. This is good because we need instruction. We have done poorly on our own and squandered what we had, as

children will. Once we held the land from the Missouri
to the Bitterroot Mountains, from the Black Hills to the
Platte, but we used it ill, you tell us. We used it only
to house and feed our people, knowing not what else
the land was for. Now it is ours no longer for you have
seen that we misused it and have taken it from us for
our own good, for you are a stern and caring father.
You have provided us instead with the cage you call
an agency and I am glad that you will be our father
and teach us how to use it for I confess to you we do
not understand how to make a living from this barren
patch upon the noble expanse that once was ours. But
as your children, you will raise us up and teach us.
Whenever a man raises anything, even a dog, he thinks
well of it, and treats it well. I see around you many
whom you have raised up and you treat them as well
as dogs. And they are grateful and lick your hand as
they should for a master must be a master and a dog a
dog.

CLARK: The man is insulting!

CROOK: Calm yourself.

CLARK: He mocks you.

CROOK: It is his manner of speaking, is it not, Gruard?
He is unaware of his irony.

GRUARD: He knows what he says and he knows how
it's heard.

CLARK: He should be arrested.

CROOK: I will receive it as hyperbole. We are here
to make peace, not to rekindle our passions. If the
message offends in general, I shall select what I like.
(*To* CRAZY HORSE) Your words are eloquent and do
me much honor. I have not the grace of tongue to
respond in kind so let me speak plainly. There is no
need to raise up the great Lakota nation. They stand in

pride and courage as tall as any on earth. I honor the Sioux and I respect them. And I am glad to hear you mention your eagerness to learn. There is much in your future, much you can learn. We will teach you to resist the winds of nature and not be blown helplessly by them. We will teach you a concept of time beyond the seasons.

We will teach you the twin horns of success, industry and ambition. You will learn to husband your animals instead of chasing them. And greatest of all, we shall teach you magic, the very greatest magic that lies in words writ down forever on the page. The word that has captured the ages and tamed them for all who will learn the simple secrets of the alphabet. Do these things and you will be free and your minds will soar on the wings of eagles throughout space throughout time, through the generations to times and places so remote they are beyond your imaginings. I, Three Stars, offer you all this, and my hand in brotherhood.

(CROOK *thrusts out his left arm.* CRAZY HORSE *stares at it.*)

WITNAKE: He must not!

(*Long pause.* CRAZY HORSE *shakes* CROOK's *hand. Thunder crashes, lightning flashes, the spirit figures appear in shock and alarm. The lights go nearly black and all exit as if a great storm is coming. Scene changes to soldiers' world. the agency at Fort Robinson. There is a table and chairs.* CLARK, CROOK *and* GRUARD *enter.*)

CROOK: I would speak with him alone, you may withdraw.

CLARK: Do you think that wise, sir? He is a dangerous man.

CROOK: Our hostilities are done. We meet now as friends.

GRUARD: You might stop chasing a bear, but if it turns to embrace you, think it over.

CROOK: Gruard, there are times when your folksiness is out of place. I will be safe alone with Crazy Horse. We have much to discuss. It is easier to establish a peace than maintain it.

CLARK: They say he is dissatisfied here and speaks openly of rebellion.

CROOK: Who says this?

GRUARD: I have heard it said.

CROOK: Have you heard it from Crazy Horse himself?

GRUARD: I am not to his current liking. He does not whisper his plots to me.

CROOK: Rumors swarm here like gnats and can drive a man as wild. Bring me only what you know, Gruard. I have no time to chase false trails.

CLARK: It is well known, sir, that Crazy Horse seeks his own agency. It chafes his pride to be under Red Cloud.

CROOK: He has been here but two weeks, he will adjust, as all men must, to the restrictions of society. Reasonable men can find accomodation to all conditions. Bid him enter.

CLARK: The guard will be outside, sir.

CROOK: Is he to think I fear him, or that he lives within a cage? We are met to discuss his new freedom—we need no guards. I am thankful for your concern, but it is misplaced. You may go.

(CLARK, GRUARD *cross towards exit.*)

GRUARD: He revels in this meeting.

CLARK: The great attract the great. They see within the other a mirror of themselves and feel most comfortable with it.

GRUARD: If I regard a mirror, when I lift my right, the left hand moves. All is backward and reversed. So may Crook find Crazy Horse. He thinks he will be talking to another civilized mind. He will meet a stone-age man. Crazy Horse will return his warmth with adamantine ignorance. The Indian reads the wind and clouds—he will accomodate ill to a library.

(They exit. Enter CRAZY HORSE.*)*

CROOK: I see you, Crazy Horse.

CRAZY HORSE: I see you, Three Stars.

CROOK: You are well met. Please, be seated.

*(*CRAZY HORSE *sits in chair, awkwardly.)*

CROOK: You are well fed?

CRAZY HORSE: The soldiers make meat for us.

CROOK: There will always be plenty of beef for you and your people. Soon you will learn to raise and herd it yourselves.

CRAZY HORSE: Herd cattle?

CROOK: You will do well once you learn how. The Apache have become excellent farmers. Last year they harvested more than twenty tons of corn and a thousand bushels of melon. This is the richest pasturage in the world. Your herds will prosper and soon you will have excess that you may trade for all you want.

CRAZY HORSE: My people want little, we have no need for trading. We need only to hunt. The soldiers tell me we may not hunt. I have not killed these soldiers, for we have a peace, but I tell you we will hunt. That is how we live.

CROOK: There are many ways to live.

CRAZY HORSE: There is but one Lakota way. The way of our fathers.

(CRAZY HORSE *stands.* CROOK *rises with some difficulty.*)

CRAZY HORSE: You are not well?

CROOK: Well enough.

CRAZY HORSE: Please, sit.

(CRAZY HORSE *sits quickly, on the floor.* CROOK *lowers himself to the floor, leaning on the chair to ease himself down.*)

CRAZY HORSE: This is better?

CROOK: This is fine, do not think on it...I am pleased you have come. There are certain laws you must make for your people.

CRAZY HORSE: Laws? We have no laws. How can I make rules for another to live by?

CROOK: You will make them together, as a people. If anyone does not obey, he can be punished.

CRAZY HORSE: If anyone does not like them he will leave and live elsewhere.

CROOK: There is no elsewhere....

CRAZY HORSE: ...What laws?

CROOK: First you must abolish the custom of slitting women's noses. There shall be no more of that.

CRAZY HORSE: If a woman sleeps with another without her husband's permission, what is the husband to do but slit her nose?

CROOK: He shall do as the Wasichu does. Cast her from him. Leave her to live on her own.

CRAZY HORSE: On her own she will die. None can live alone. Is it a crime to die for, to sleep with another? She can live with a slit nose, but not without people.

CROOK: It must stop. Also in grief, your people must cease to disfigure themselves. Slashing of limbs, self-amputation—this too must stop.

CRAZY HORSE: Would you not give the joint of a finger for a loved one? What else have I to give that is truly mine?

CROOK: It is not grief, it is the display of grief. You may continue to cut your hair and paint your face, that is display enough.

CRAZY HORSE: And these are the laws we will "make together as a people"?

CROOK: The ways of freedom must first be taught. If you see your child crawl towards a fire, do you not stop him?

CRAZY HORSE: I do not. He must learn the danger for himself.

CROOK: You could save him pain.

CRAZY HORSE: The pain teaches with instruction that lasts. A man truly learns only those lessons he teaches himself.

CROOK: We do not believe it is necessary to learn everything anew. A self-taught man has oft a fool for instructor. It is not necessary for each man to re-invent the wheel.

CRAZY HORSE: It is not necessary to invent the wheel at all. Our ponies can drag all we need.

CROOK: Before you had the horse you carried only what your dogs and women could drag. Once the horse was yours, you found a greater weight to pull. With the wheel and cart you will find even more.

CRAZY HORSE: More what? We have what we need.

CROOK: But you could have more.

CRAZY HORSE: The wheel can not go where we would travel.

CROOK: Then make roads.

CRAZY HORSE: Why should we make roads we do not need for wheels we do not need to pull more of what we do not need?

CROOK: If you had the wheels you would need the roads to pull all that you could, because once acquired, you would need it. Accumulation is human nature.

CRAZY HORSE: Shall I eat more to grow fat that I might eat more?

CROOK: Excess is the essence of civilization. Just enough is not enough for growth. (*He shifts positions.*)

CRAZY HORSE: ...You are uncomfortable.

CROOK: No.

CRAZY HORSE: Would you stand?

(CRAZY HORSE *stands.* CROOK *tries to get up, with difficulty.*)

CROOK: If you desire.

(CRAZY HORSE *solicitously sits again.* CROOK *is half way up. He cranks himself down again.*)

CRAZY HORSE: It is for you to say.

CROOK: It is no matter. There is no relief.... Of these laws...

CRAZY HORSE: If I give my people these unnatural strictures, will you allow us to hunt?

CROOK: It is forbidden you should leave the agency to hunt. The fathers in Washington fear it. They do not know you as I do. They do not understand that the Lakota lives by his honor and that if you say you will go only to hunt and then return, you will return.

CRAZY HORSE: It is not the Lakota who breaks promises. You will tell them.

CROOK: I have tried. They do not—they will not know you. But there is a way. Your enemy, the Nez Perce (*N B: pronounced Nez Purse*) has broken from his agency and flees toward Grandmother's Land to the North that we call Canada. They are led by Chief Joseph. They must cross Lakota territory to reach the border. If you would scout for us to stop the Nez Perce, I could tell the fathers of your cooperation.

(CRAZY HORSE *gets to his feet in agitation, forgetting* CROOK's *disability. During* CRAZY HORSE's *speech,* CROOK *gets to his feet again.*)

CROOK: They are your enemy.

CRAZY HORSE: I have slain the Nez Perce where I have found them and their hair adorns my lance and lodge. Yet I fought them but to kill them. The Wasichu would erase them.

CROOK: We would but return them to the agency.

CRAZY HORSE: We kill our enemies, warrior and woman alike if we can. We do not send them disease, we do not give them the burning cup to make fools of them, we do not starve them and leave them without the land. We just kill them.

CROOK: Think on it. If you assist us in this matter, I shall assist you.

CRAZY HORSE: I like neither the look nor smell of it. Will thinking change it?

(CRAZY HORSE *sits on floor.* CROOK *makes his arduous way back down.*)

CRAZY HORSE: It is a wound?

CROOK: The decay of years. The spine is pinching on a nerve.

CRAZY HORSE: You have a spirit in the leg.

CROOK: It is some days more spirited than others.

CRAZY HORSE: Sit thus.

(CRAZY HORSE *lies back, supporting himself on his elbows, arching his back.* CROOK *emulates him. This position affords him some relief and* CROOK *sighs in gratitude.*)

CRAZY HORSE: (*Of Chair*) It is unnatural to sit upon a chair. You need a buffalo robe to recline on. I shall send you mine and a shaman to rid you of the spirit.

CROOK: The robe would be welcome and the shaman is fair exchange. Missionaries will be visiting you soon enough.

CRAZY HORSE: The Bible men? I will not have them among my people. They tell lies and cause distress.

CROOK: There is no escape from the priests, my friend. I can not avoid them, nor can you. Do as I, nod and close your ears.

CRAZY HORSE: You do not listen to your priests?

CROOK: I pray you, keep this knowledge to yourself. It is most impolitic to admit to a free mind in religion. A leader must wave piety like a banner and embrace hypocrisy in matters godly. In religion as cuisine, simple tastes prevail among the many. They like the old favorites.

CRAZY HORSE: You say your Bible God is false?

CROOK: No falser than another; nor truer. Think me a man of thought which is to say a man of doubts. There may be those who speak to God, he does not speak to me.

CRAZY HORSE: He speaks to me. I have heard his voice, I have seen him.

CROOK: What does he look like?

CRAZY HORSE: Very old. Older than the oldest grandfather, yet strong.

CROOK: That accords well enough with Christian thought, a stern old man with lightning bolt in hand.

CRAZY HORSE: Yes! I have seen him hurl the lightning. He has brought forth the thunder and unleashed the rain.

CROOK: God as weather, fire and storm. You will do well as a Christian.

CRAZY HORSE: Christian! Would you take the Great Spirit from us?

CROOK: Grow him a beard, man, and the priests will never know the difference.

CRAZY HORSE: There is but one Great Spirit, he is not Washichu!

CROOK: Your prayers will avail you as well be they addressed to the Great Spirit or Jehovah, they go to the same void. Your God will understand.

CRAZY HORSE: He will not hear Wasichu prayer! There must be dance, there must be chant! It must be done the Lakota way. That is the way it is, that is the way it has always been. The Great Spirit has given these ways to the People. (*Rises*) We will perish beyond recall without the Great Spirit, and he without us. We are one, as the buffalo and the grass are one.

CROOK: People do not perish without god, I assure you.
  The sun will shine and rain will fall on the devoted and the atheist alike.

CRAZY HORSE: Then the godless partake as scavengers at the feast of others. All our lives are filled with the Spirits, we eat and breathe with them, as they would have us do. And if we stop, there comes the chaos to engulf us all.

CROOK: You truly believe this?

CRAZY HORSE: I do not believe it. It is so. That is why we must never abandon the ways of the Lakota.

(CROOK *stands with difficulty.*)

CRAZY HORSE: Do not stand if it pains you.

CROOK: It is neither the standing nor the sitting but the ride between the two. If we could perhaps dispense with this bouncing courtesy.

CRAZY HORSE: As you will.

CROOK: Your relationship to your god concerns not me. It is the men of the cloth who will show you least tolerance. Heed them or not, as you will. Our mythology is the least we have to offer. There are many valued gifts we shall proffer you.

CRAZY HORSE: We do not need your gifts.

CROOK: You have taken much from us already. You were quick to master the rifle and the horse.

CRAZY HORSE: The horse was given to the Lakota by Buffalo Woman. That is known by all. She came in the form of a virgin, riding the great ancestor of all horses, which is why all horses today belong to the Lakota. It is known by all.

CROOK: Your knife, your axe blades, your cooking pots, even the heads of your arrows are shaped from metals dug from American soil, heated with coal and char from New England forests and forged with American muscles.

CRAZY HORSE: We have lived without these things.

CROOK: Not in your lifetime. Nor can you return to an age before convenience. Why do your women put an iron pot straight to the flame rather than dropping heated stones into the buffalo paunch? Why do they cut wood with a blade of metal instead of flint? Time

is a flood that courses only one way, you can not turn
it round nor swim upstream. There is but one way to
survive a flood. You must swim with it. Let the power
of its current buoy and propel you forth.

CRAZY HORSE: I am no fish.

CROOK: No, you are a man and it is given you to
live in this hour, not another. Now is the hour of the
American. You are not merely a Lakota, you are a
human, you are a man with infinite capacity to think
and dream and aspire. You learned once to hunt with a
bow and eat the raw liver of your chase, you were not
born this way, you learned it. You are still young, now
learn another way and lead your people on the new
path to freedom.

CRAZY HORSE: You speak of freedom? We have lived
freely upon our land before you came. You have stolen
our land and penned us onto agencies. This land is
ours, given us by the Great Spirit. It is the land of our
fathers' fathers' fathers.

CROOK: Land is never stolen. It can not be lifted and
removed. Land is occupied. Land is utilized. It is tilled,
it is fenced, it is settled. It belongs to those who possess
it fully. The Sioux have no claim to this land of more
than a century. It is the land of your father's father, but
little more. The Sioux were not west of the Missouri
before the last century, pushed here by the Ojibway
and you in turn propelled the resident Crow and
Shoshone into the mountains and the colder climes.
They, too, claimed a gift of the Great Spirit, no doubt,
but you see you did not heed it.

CRAZY HORSE: I know nothing of this.

CROOK: (*Touches a book*) It is here. All history is here,
writ large for those who will see. There is a sweep of
things over time, a grand design that must be filled.
Standing close we can not see the forest and think it

only trees, but from a height and from a distance it has a shape and scope and limit; and so with history whose purpose is bedimmed as events swirl about us. Only atop the mountain of time can we see its relentless purpose. History is not right. It is not wrong. It is inevitable. It shapes us all as the water shapes the rock. Be you recalcitrant as stone, you will respond to it in time. My own people, the Britons, once lived like you, without the wheel, without the word. We dressed in skins and daubed ourselves with indigo and prayed to slabs of granite. Today Britain waves its colors over Asia, Africa, the Levant. We did not ask the world to stop, we learned to turn it to our own desire. We put aside our old ways, as has every people that would advance. What difference now between Saxon and Norman? Who mourns today the vanished Visigoth?

CRAZY HORSE: I know nothing of your "history".

CROOK: Crazy Horse is a wise man. A wise man knows when the sun has fallen. And when a new one rises. Though there lies between us the chasm of ages, we shall leap the gap in a generation. Your children will be Americans and step from the Stone age to modern times with the ease of the elk vaulting a summer brook.

   We will give you schools that your young may learn Wasichu ways, that they might travel to our great cities and speak our tongue and be accepted everywhere. People from the wide world have come to this land. The wise ones learn to do as we do and they are welcomed and their young are as free as ours. Those who would cling to roots long severed wither and fall from the vine. If a man is forced to live in the air he would do well to learn the ways of the birds.

CRAZY HORSE: Our children shall not be birds. They are Lakota.

CROOK: Lakota, yes. Americans, too. Lakota—
Americans.

CRAZY HORSE: Lakotas. Do you need more Wasichus?
I am told you have people without number. Why must
you make whites of our children?

CROOK: (*Pause.*) Your children will learn the ways of
the Americans and can choose whether to live with the
wheel or without.

CRAZY HORSE: You would teach them in these schools
to live like Wasichus? Wear your clothes, speak your
language, herd your cattle?

CROOK: I would have them live in the world that is
around them.

CRAZY HORSE: And when I wear your clothes and eat
your food and speak your tongue, what part of me
remains Lakotah?

CROOK: You would be Lakotah though you dressed in
silk to take communion.

CRAZY HORSE: I bid you come to my camp and take
into your hands a Lakotah babe and hold that child
and see its face and feel its warmth and let it grasp
your finger. Then I will tell you how that child is called
so that when next we speak you can put a name to
these children who will be taken forever from the land
that loves them and ripped from the arms of their
ancestors and barred forever from the ways that have
been given to them since time began.

CROOK: I offer the gifts of our society in friendship and
concern. Will you think on them?

CRAZY HORSE: If offered in friendship, I must consider
them.

CROOK: And the pursuit of the Nez Perce, will you
think on that as well? It will help your people.

CRAZY HORSE: If you say it will help my people, then I must think on that also.

CROOK: Good. (*In conclusion*) So. It is well done.

CRAZY HORSE: (*Stops him*) Now I would give you a gift.

CROOK: It is not necessary.

CRAZY HORSE: You have offered much—I will give more in return.

You tell me you have no god, no great creator. I mourn for you for such a loss. I know why this is. Your life has grown too complex and pulled you away from simple truth. You must learn to see again. In the morning, rise, before the light, and go alone to the prairie, then watch at sunup as the earth comes to life. See the world stir, hear the insects wake, the wind quicken. Watch the very grass straighten and reach for the sun. Taste the grass, wash its dew upon your skin, inhale the scents of the land. All that you see and hear and taste and feel is god. The Lakota god, the god of our land. I give you god in the morning. To share with us. I have no greater gift.... Will you think on it?

CROOK: (*Touched*) I will think much on it.

(CROOK *Advances to shake hands. but has a sudden crisis with his leg and back. he grips the table.* CRAZY HORSE *sees this, starts to help. then decides that the best thing is not to embarrass* CROOK.)

CRAZY HORSE: I must leave you now. I am not well. I sleep but little and your diet is hard for my bowel. I must lie down. (*Grips stomach*)

CROOK: (*With difficulty*) Of course. Please take care of yourself. Your health is most important. I shall send my surgeon to see you.

CRAZY HORSE: And I, the shaman. Perhaps we shall cure each other.

CROOK: And you will think on it?

CRAZY HORSE: (*Pause.*) I must.

(CRAZY HORSE *exits.* CLARK *enters hurriedly.*)

CLARK: Sir, I have a message from General Sheridan....

CROOK: (*In pain*) The chair!

(CLARK *quickly brings chair to* CROOK *who eases into it.*)

CLARK: Are you all right, sir?

CROOK: You have a message from Sheridan. Would you keep it from me? Speak.

CLARK: The Apaches have broken from the agencies again.

CROOK: No! Why? They prospered there! What man would go against his own advantage? (*Pause*) Who leads them?

CLARK: ...Geronimo.

CROOK: The devil! His people have a better life yet he, for spite—for spite! —would suck them all again within the chaos of the past...Geronimo!

CLARK: General Sheridan desires you to hasten to the Department of Arizona and return the Apache to their agency.

CROOK: Yes, by God! Though he crawl beneath a rock I will grub him out and haul him back to peace by his scalp. (*He moves, is brought up short by the pain in his leg.*)

CROOK: Geronimo lies a thousand miles to the south...A thousand miles astride a mule.

CLARK: If General Sheridan knew of your condition...

CROOK: I have no "condition". ...But, ahh, I am weary, Clark. I have spent my majority with the Indians. I have grown old in my work to liberate them.

CLARK: You are not old, sir.

CROOK: I feel it, son. I feel it like a weakness in the
bone. I have given them my prime, the Paiutes, the
Apache, the Sioux. They have loved me but little for it.
...Tell me, Clark, have I done wrong?

CLARK: Of course not, sir.

CROOK: Could I have done otherwise?

CLARK: Only by doing worse. You know what is best
for them.

CROOK: For Christ's sweet sake, Lieutenant, I do not
know best! I can not read the future! I see it looming
there like a thundercloud, but I can not read it. I draw
over-heavy on reason, I strain its uses. Religion is not
"reasonable", nor hope, nor love, yet how men cling
to them. Crazy Horse is a man incarnadine with the
blood of his enemies, yet when he offered a plea for his
people's life, he bid me hold a babe...I am not fitted for
this task.

CLARK: It has been magnificent work. You have made
the country safe for settlement. You have blunted the
threat of the Indian and penned him in.

CROOK: Do you still not understand? If confinement
were all, any jailer would do as well. I do not seek to
diminish them, I want to expand them, Clark. They
die apace, I know that, they know that. From the
Atlantic to here and the western shore we have pushed
them and slain them and herded them before us like
sheep. They have died of the pox, they have died of
alcohol, they have died of sorrow and shame. We have
occupied their land and we have bought their home
for beads and bottles and cloth. I know this and they
know this. But tell me, Clark, how could it have been
otherwise? There is not a house on this continent that
does not rest on land that once was theirs. Which of
our cities would you give up? Which could we spare?
Our people are like a woman gravid with child; when

her water bursts, she can not hold back the birthing, the child will be born whether the mother will it or no. We are such a people, we will be born upon this land. It is inevitable, Clark, and if a thing is inevitable, it is neither right nor wrong. It must be. If you have bread and I have none and you leave yours upon the table to mold and rot, what shall I do? Watch it green and fuzz? I shall eat it, Clark, and so would you and so would any other, white, Indian or Hindu. Their day is over, a babe could see it. I offer them civilization but they do not want it. Yet can I leave them three thousand years behind? Would they cling to "the old ways" a century from now? Two centuries? It is over! As if there were something grand and noble to wrap yourself in the cloak of your ancestors and stifle there forever. Nothing in this world is as it was two hundred years ago. Or one hundred. Or even fifty...I know no better way than what I have done... But Lord, I grow weary... Summon the staff, I must make plans to leave for Arizona within the week.

CLARK: What of Crazy Horse, sir?

CROOK: He will allow me to save him. He is no Geronimo. We shall make him chief of all the Apaches.

CLARK: Lakota, sir.

CROOK: What say you?

CLARK: You confused the Lakota with the Apache.

CROOK: No. I did not. Send Gruard to inform Crazy Horse we meet again tomorrow.

(CROOK, CLARK, GUARD *exit.* CRAZY HORSE *enters on the rise to tormented, disturbing dream music. Bars surround him, he is encaged, one of his own people holds his arm as he tries to break through the bars. The spirits appear above him, reaching down a hand to pull him free. He reaches for the hand but the dream fades as* WITNAKE *enters.)*

CRAZY HORSE: I was encircled by reason and here is the most practical man.

WITNAKE: I have heard what Three Stars offers you. May I give you counsel?

CRAZY HORSE: As the wolf may give counsel to the fawn.

WITNAKE: I am still and always your brother, Crazy Horse.

CRAZY HORSE: My mother will be alarmed to hear it.

WITNAKE: You must do as Three Stars bids you.

CRAZY HORSE: The Wasichus have kept no promises before this.

WITNAKE: It is our only chance, they can now erase us. We must trust them.

CRAZY HORSE: When has a Lakotah feared a death that is but our passage to the other side?

WITNAKE: I do not fear to die in battle—but my wife is again with child, my only son has but two years—if I could die to protect them I would take my own life on the instant—but history is sterner. My death will not protect them against this enemy. I must sacrifice now by surviving to protect them.

CRAZY HORSE: Their lives will not be worth the living if they are not true Lakotahs.

WITNAKE: ...and yet, I see other men who live their lives, loving women, raising sons, dancing and sweating in the sun and lifting a child in their arms for all the world as if they found some joy and honor in life though they were not People...There are times when the fearless mood is upon the buffalo and we can ride within a lance thrust before they start, and there are times when they will race upon the sight of man. At those times we must sneak upon the herd, skins of wolves upon our back to hide our humanity. We have learned to suit our methods to their moods; now the world has turned as willful as the herd and we must learn a new way to deal with it.

CRAZY HORSE: We are one with the buffalo, they love us as we love them and die gladly that we may live. The Wasichu love us not.

WITNAKE: Then let us be cunning. Let us cloak ourselves in some small scrap of Washichu ways. It is simple enough and can do no harm. You see, I wear this trinket.

(WITNAKE *reveals a crucifix.* CRAZY HORSE *recoils.*) It is a trifle, yet pleases them so.

(GRUARD *enters.*)

GRUARD: I see you, Crazy Horse, I see you, Witnake.

WITNAKE: I see you, Gruard.

CRAZY HORSE: I do not see you. (*He turns his head away from* GRUARD.)

GRUARD: Can you hear me, then?

CRAZY HORSE: I do not hear you.

GRUARD: You will hear me because I speak with the roar of Three Stars. His voice is my voice and his message is this: You will meet with him tomorrow and give him answer.

CRAZY HORSE: I have told him I would think on it.

GRUARD: He does not accept that answer.

CRAZY HORSE: He does not accept the word of Crazy Horse!

GRUARD: You will have a day to sulk within your lodge, and then tomorrow you will answer yes.

CRAZY HORSE: He dares to speak of me in this manner! He thinks me a child!?

GRUARD: He thinks you a man—who acts like a child.

(CRAZY HORSE *grabs* GRUARD, *puts knife to his throat.*)

CRAZY HORSE: Is this the strength of a child?

WITNAKE: You must not! He speaks for Three Stars!

CRAZY HORSE: Three Stars' words offend me. This will silence his voice.

WITNAKE: The soldiers will kill us all!

(WITNAKE *wrestles* CRAZY HORSE *off of* GRUARD.)

CRAZY HORSE: (*Brandishing knife*) I will meet with Three Stars.
 Let him come here, within my lodge and I shall give him the same answer I give you, Gruard. I shall feast him with tongue and heart that have a most familiar taste! (*He exits.*)

GRUARD: He will cause you much trouble. If Three Stars is threatened there will be no peace except the grave.

WITNAKE: He was angry, he spoke his heart, not his mind.

GRUARD: For Crazy Horse they are always the same. There should be a split twixt head and heart especially in the time of talk. You and I know that. Words must come from the mind, shaped for cunning and advantage. If a humble word buys an extra beef and a blanket for your son, it is the way of wisdom—it is the way of the Wasichu.

WITNAKE: He is our chief, the greatest of our chiefs.

GRUARD: He is a chief for war. In a time of peace he is no more use than a wounded bear, raging for revenge. ...You would do better without him, Witnake.

WITNAKE: The People will never replace him.

GRUARD: The People are sometimes slow to know their own advantage. There are always those who more swiftly understand—and they must swiftly act... If Three Stars is timely warned of Crazy Horse's threat...

WITNAKE: I think he meant it not.

GRUARD: If Three Stars is told of what he said, let Crook parse it as he will, it would look well if a Lakota do the telling. Much favor would befall such a man—and his family. But if Crazy Horse should live his angry words, the Wasichu cattle on which your children dine will vanish and you will feast on vengeance and the air.... You have a son—I did also. Mine is gone but your own paternity can instruct you in my grief, just as mine can make me fearful for the loss of your boy. Crazy Horse is a great man—the plains are strewn with bodies of Lakota and foe alike to prove it—but there are times for greatness to blaze and ignite the prairies, and there are times when a campfire is all that men require. These are subtler times. The wind has shifted and the flames of greatness are now licking at the lodges where the helpless ones lie sleeping. Choler and pride will not quench a fire, they will feed it. It requires no leader to douse a blaze, but men with willing hands who prize that which they would not have consumed...

WITNAKE: (*Pause*) He can not change. That is his greatness. ...That is our curse.

GRUARD: Then you do know it.— Will you walk with me awhile... brother?

(WITNAKE *exits with* GRUARD)

(*Enter* CROOK *with* SOLDIERS.)

CROOK: Be doubly certain the books are well packed and the trunk then sealed with resin. We have many rivers to cross and I will not have the world's treasures soaked in prairie water. Pack them all save Shakespeare. The bard travels well, he shall ride with me upon my saddle.

(CLARK *enters hurriedly,* SOLDIERS *exit.*)

CLARK: Sir! Thank God you have not yet left for your meeting with Crazy Horse.

CROOK: I leave within the hour.

CLARK: Sir, you must not. There is grave danger there.

CROOK: Again you would have me fear the man? Clark, we have met, we have talked, you see me intact.

CLARK: I have intelligence. (*Gestures to others*) These men have heard him say he will kill you.

(*Enter* GRUARD *and* WITNAKE.)

CROOK: Heard him? You heard him say this, Gruard? Tell me what you know, man.

GRUARD: I went to fetch him for today as you bade me. The "great chief" was in his choler and said that you should come to him and he would kill you.

CROOK: He meant otherwise. They do much speak in metaphor. (*Aside, to* CLARK) This tale is much too plain and not at all of Gruard's mode. I do not like it.

CLARK: I believe him, sir.

CROOK: You yourself did warn me not to trust him. Have you changed or has he? And if it be you who judged him wrong at first, how shall I value your judgment now?

CLARK: It is clearly treason, sir. We must arrest him before he acts. It is a threat not only to you but to the United States of America. You represent the government, sir.

CROOK: (*Sharply*) I know my status, Clark.... It is but one man's word.

GRUARD: This man heard him, sir.

CLARK: Come forward.

GRUARD: This man is Witnake, General. He leads our Lakota scouts.

CROOK: I know this man.

GRUARD: He was present when Crazy Horse threatened your life. He heard it and can relate it as it happened.

CROOK: Then let him. Is this story true, Witnake? Did you hear Crazy Horse vow to take my life?

WITNAKE: He did say so.

CLARK: You see!

CROOK: The words, he may have said the words. But did he mean it? You were there. He is your chief.

WITNAKE: He is the greatest of our chiefs.

CROOK: All the more reason to speak with the greatest care. Grave consequences may devolve from your testimony.
    Do you understand this?

WITNAKE: ...What will become of him?

CLARK: That is not your concern. Speak the truth.

WITNAKE: (*To* GRUARD) I will not have him harmed.

GRUARD: No harm will come to him, but much to the tribe if you do not speak.

CROOK: We do not harm men for their speech, Witnake. But Crazy Horse is the leader of thousands. When he speaks, his voice echoes like thunder and the Lakota resonate with his words. A man may yell shrilly in exuberance—or in anger. From a distance it is hard to distinguish the whoops of joy from cries of rage. I must know his mind. You were there. Was there fury in Crazy Horse's voice?

GRUARD: He is a Lakota warrior, he will speak the truth—as he would have his son do.

CROOK: Be still, Gruard...Witnake? Did you see fury? Did you hear it?

WITNAKE: ...There was fury in the tent.

CROOK: (*Disappointed*) Very well. You may go.

(GRUARD, WITNAKE *cross to exit.*)

WITNAKE: (*To* GRUARD) They will not harm him?

GRUARD: You have preserved the future.

(GRUARD, WITNAKE *exit.*)

CLARK: We must arrest Crazy Horse, sir.

CROOK: It is not clear. His speech was hesitant, there was no conviction there.

CLARK: Gruard was clear enough.

CROOK: I met the man within this tent, we spoke of policy and gods and if there was heat between us it was no more than the friction of opposing ideas strongly held. He feigned illness to save my face with more natural diplomacy than all of Washington assembled. If Crazy Horse speaks treason, I will believe it from his lips alone. You shall fetch him, Clark. Take three men, no more, and make no move to alarm him. But do not fail to bring him in, Lieutenant. I will not have him slip into the wilds again.

CLARK: He would be more dangerous than Geronimo, sir. We would war another year at least.

CROOK: Go and fetch the man. With great civility. He is their supreme chief and I would not offend him or his people. He is not under arrest, nor shall he be unless he write the warrant with his own hand. Go, but softly.

(CLARK *exits;* CROOK *tries to stretch his bad leg.*)

CROOK: If it would end the pain I would saw off the leg myself. (*Calling*) Soldier! Continue to pack. Do not forget the bard. (*He exits.*)

(*The spirit figures remove their native dress and don Wasichu clothing and hats.* CRAZY HORSE *tries to stop them but can not. Slowly the spirits withdraw, and* CRAZY HORSE *can not stop that, either. The bars of prison clash in front of* CRAZY HORSE *again. The dream ends and all exit.*)

(CROOK *enters, sits at his table.* CRAZY HORSE *enters.*)

CROOK: I see you, Crazy Horse.

CRAZY HORSE: I see you, Three Stars. You are well?

CROOK: I am well, I thank you. And you are no longer indisposed?

CRAZY HORSE: I? ...Oh. It was a small thing—though ill enough at the time. Your surgeon came to see me, as you said. He found nothing wrong. The man is a fool. Were I summoned to a chief I would find as much awry as the chief desired. To do otherwise is insult.

CROOK: The surgeon is yet young and learns his craft.

CRAZY HORSE: Did my shaman serve you well?

CROOK: An excellent man. He found me beset with spirits.

CRAZY HORSE: He is very good. Our best.

CROOK: He treated me with tooth and feather and chanted past an hour.

CRAZY HORSE: An excellent man. I am pleased you are well.

CROOK: It is good we have a chance to speak again before I go. We have matters to resolve which I would not leave undone behind.

CRAZY HORSE: You are leaving?

CROOK: I must to the Apache for a time.

CRAZY HORSE: Your heart is often there. You may
count again their bushels of corn. They will hold their
melons in the air that you may bless them.

CROOK: I am glad your humor is benign. (*Aside*) (There
is no treason here, he lacks the serpent's guile.) I would
not leave you yet, our business thus undone, but I am
so bid by a higher chief.

CRAZY HORSE: Who will take your place?

CROOK: Lieutenant Clark for a time, then others.

CRAZY HORSE: If you leave us we shall suffer more.
You wish us well where others may not.

CROOK: You know this of me?

CRAZY HORSE: I believe this. You do not understand us,
but you respect us.

CROOK: Others who follow me will not understand
you at all. They may not honor the Lakota as I do, you
must start now with my guidance upon the right path.
You will not be led astray as others might. Have you
thought on the matters we discussed?

CRAZY HORSE: I have.

CROOK: The Nez Perce have crossed the Snake. They
will be on Lakota land within the week. I would not
have them reach Grandmother's land. Will you lead
the scouts? (*Pause*) Much good will come to you.
(*Pause*) I can tell those who follow me that Crazy Horse
has cooperated in every way. You will have your own
agency. (*Pause*) Let me help you, man. I have seen how
others treat you, it is a base and ignoble history, they
will send in men who have not fought you, have not
known you, have not admired you, they will send in
men who see you only at the agency with your hands
stretched out in importunity. Embrace what I offer, it is
the best there is, and let me then trumpet to my nation,
Crazy Horse has changed! Crazy Horse would lead his

people to the future. Let me tell them, once, for god's sake this once, treat the Lakota as our brothers for they are truly willing to be so! Take it, man, take it!

CRAZY HORSE: *(Pause)* I will find the Nez Perce for you...

CROOK: Excellent!

CRAZY HORSE: ...if you will grant me a favor in return.

CROOK: Granted. Name it.

CRAZY HORSE: No schools.

CROOK: What?

CRAZY HORSE: Your schools are graveyards for all that is Lakota. Our children will learn the Wasichu ways and the Spirits will perish and the ancestors will lose all power. I will do as you bid if you promise me there will be no schools. No books.

CROOK: No schools? That is the best I have to give you!

CRAZY HORSE: We do not want it.

CROOK: Then you know not its value. I offer you the greatest of our treasures. Take it, embrace it, wrap yourself in this vestment of Wasichu culture. Education will shield you and protect you and warm you.

CRAZY HORSE: We will become Wasichu.

CROOK: Man, there is nothing else left to become—but extinct.

CRAZY HORSE: If we are to be the last of the Lakota, then we shall die as Lakota.

CROOK: Pride? You do this for pride?

CRAZY HORSE: I do this for the Spirits, I do it for our ancestors.

CROOK: You would doom generations yet unborn for your pride?

CRAZY HORSE: I would preserve their pride, for they are lost without it.

CROOK: I beg you reconsider. The world is grown too small, you can not live alone. Your only hope is to join us.

CRAZY HORSE: Then we shall live without hope. But not without pride.

CROOK: I beg you.

CRAZY HORSE: We shall teach our own what they must know.

CROOK: You do not know what they must know. It is a different world, yours is gone.

CRAZY HORSE: The sky is the same. And the grass.

CROOK: The grass will change. Wheat is also grass, and corn. I beg you.

CRAZY HORSE: No schools.

CROOK: (*Holding book*) Take this much. This is the greatest gift, the greatest magic. The mind of another, preserved forever. Take this much at least; it is knowledge.

CRAZY HORSE: Knowledge of your world poisons our very air. Without guns, without whiskey, without disease, still would that knowledge destroy us.

CROOK: (*Giving up*) I can not protect you more. I must leave.

CRAZY HORSE: Go to the Apache. Make Wasichu of them—and tell them then of the Lakota who remain.

(CRAZY HORSE *exits.* CLARK *enters.*)

CLARK: Did it go well, sir?

CROOK: We wrestle in the dark, Crazy Horse and I, and I fear we grapple not each other but the darkness.

CLARK: Your escort is ready, sir.

CROOK: I can not leave him behind, Clark. His resistance will suppurate and burst upon the tribe.

CLARK: What would you have me do with him? (*Pause*) Sir?

CROOK: (*Pause*) He will leave the agency when he can bear it no more. Already his patience is thread bare. And when he goes, many will follow.

CLARK: Another Geronimo.

CROOK: He has done no wrong, but willfully refuses to do right.... If he is removed, they are broken.

CLARK: They are broken already.

CROOK: No. They are defeated, they are not broken as long as the will of Crazy Horse binds them. But his will is to lead them into annihilation.

(SOLDIER *enters, comes to attention.*)

CROOK: (*To* SOLDIER) I'm coming.

(SOLDIER *exits*)

CLARK: What shall I do, sir?

CROOK: Crazy Horse must not leave the agency.

CLARK: The agency is many miles, there are no fences, no guards....

CROOK: He must not leave it.... How can I leave this burden to you? ...We have served a campaign together, you and I, but I know not your heart in this matter. Tell me, Lieutenant, how will you treat them?

CLARK: With dignity, sir. And civility. I know they are not beggars lest we make them so.

CROOK: Good. Then I shall leave them without fear.

CLARK: Yes, sir. (*Salutes*)

CROOK: (*Handshake.*) Farewell, Clark.

CLARK: Goodbye, sir.

(CROOK *exits. Pause.* GRUARD *enters.*)

GRUARD: So we've seen the last of that limp, have we?

CLARK: While I command, Gruard, you will speak no ill of General Crook.

GRUARD: I didn't mean to slur your hero.

CLARK: There are no heroes, Gruard. Only those who strive and those who don't. Fetch the man Witnake. I would have you bring Crazy Horse close to hand... Bring him gently, Gruard.

(CLARK, GRUARD *exit as* CRAZY HORSE *enters on rise.* WITNAKE *enters.*)

WITNAKE: White Hat Clark bids you come to see him, cousin.

CRAZY HORSE: Shall I live with the Washichus? They bid me come every day. Tell White Hat it is not my pleasure to come.

WITNAKE: Our rations are cut, cousin. They say you will not cooperate...We wish you to cooperate.

(*Enter* GRUARD. *He stands ominously, waiting. Indians appear, also waiting ominously.* CRAZY HORSE *looks about, slowly falls in beside* WITNAKE, GRUARD. WITNAKE *and* GRUARD *walk on either side of* CRAZY HORSE. *They cross from the rise to the lower stage. Spirit figures appear on rise. Eerie music*)

CRAZY HORSE: Feel the heat upon your skin. Summer comes, cousin. The land will swarm again with buffalo and the bees shall make honey in the wood. Our land is so beautiful in summer. Shall we ride out today to the prairie? Shall we dance our gratitude to the powers for giving us this bountiful land?...

(SOLDIER *enters with rifle and bayonet.* CRAZY HORSE *reacts to him with alarm.*)

CRAZY HORSE: What place is this? Where is White Hat Clark?

WITNAKE: He is coming.

(The bars of a jail are projected behind CRAZY HORSE. *He turns, sees the bars.)*

CRAZY HORSE: No! *(He pulls a knife.)*

GRUARD: Guard!

WITNAKE: No, cousin!

*(*WITNAKE *grabs* CRAZY HORSE *from behind, trying to restrain him from causing a disaster.)*

CRAZY HORSE: Stand aside!

GRUARD: He's escaping! Guard! He's escaping!

*(*CLARK *enters, steps forward to stop* SOLDIER, *too late.)*

CLARK: Guard!

*(*SOLIDER *steps forward and bayonets* CRAZY HORSE, *still held by* WITNAKE, *in the side. The others pull back as* CRAZY HORSE *sinks to the ground. Spirit figures, on the rise, looking down at* CRAZY HORSE, *begin to withdraw.)*

CLARK: *(Angrily, to* GRUARD*)* I did not wish this!

GRUARD: He brought it on himself.

CLARK: *(To* CRAZY HORSE*)* I did not wish this.

CRAZY HORSE: Is this more of Three Star's "history"?

CLARK: *(To guard)* Fetch the surgeon!

CRAZY HORSE: *(To* WITNAKE*)* The flood is upon us. I can swim no more. You must save them.

WITNAKE: What flood, cousin?

CRAZY HORSE: *(Dying, begins to chant)* Hey a hey...

(Spirits exit.)

CRAZY HORSE: Hey a hey...

(CROOK *mounts rise where spirits had previously appeared.*
the lights of the spirits fade and vanish forever.)

CRAZY HORSE: Grandfathers? (*Pause. Dying*) I am cold,
Grandfathers.

(CRAZY HORSE *dies.* CROOK *stands upon the rise, looking*
mournfully down at CRAZY HORSE. *The music of a single*
Indian drum and rattle are heard, then they, too, die.)

(*Blackout*)

END OF PLAY